Multiple Intelligences

GRADE 6

teaching kids the way they learn

written by
Nomi J. Waldman

Cover by Dawn Devries Sokol

Interior illustrations by Scott Bricher and Don O'Connor

Symbol design by Rose Sheifer

FS-23285 Multiple Intelligences: Teaching Kids the Way They Learn Grade 6

All rights reserved. Printed in the U.S.A.

Copyright © 1999 Frank Schaffer Publications, Inc.

23740 Hawthorne Blvd., Torrance, CA 90505

TABLE of CONTENTS

What Is the Multiple Intelligences Theory?

The Multiple Intelligences Theory, developed and researched by Dr. Howard Gardner, recognizes the multifaceted profile of the human mind. In his book *Frames of Mind* (Basic Books, 1993) Dr. Gardner explains that every human possesses several intelligences in greater or lesser degrees. Each person is born with a unique intelligence profile and uses any or all of these intelligences to acquire knowledge and experience.

At present Gardner has defined eight intelligences. Below are the intelligences and a simplified definition of each. A more complete explanation of each intelligence is found at the end of the introduction.

- verbal-linguistic: word intelligence
- logical-mathematical: number and reasoning intelligence
- visual-spatial: picture intelligence
- musical-rhythmic: music and rhythm intelligence
- bodily-kinesthetic: body intelligence
- interpersonal: social intelligence
- intrapersonal: self intelligence
- naturalist: natural environment intelligence

Gardner stresses that although intelligence is a biological function, it is inseparable from the cultural context in which it exists. He cites the example of Bobby Fischer, the chess champion. In a culture without chess, Fischer would not have been able to become a good chess player.

The Multiple Intelligences Theory in the Classroom

The Multiple Intelligences Theory has been making its way into the educational setting over the past decade. Instinctively, educators have recognized that their students learn differently, respond uniquely to a variety of teaching techniques, and have their individual preferences. Traditional educational programs do not recognize the unique intelligence profile of each student. Traditionally educators have operated according to the belief that there is a single type of intelligence, based on a combination of math and verbal ability. This more one-dimensional view gave rise to the commonly held definition of an "IQ." According to this definition, all individuals are born with this general ability and it does not change with age, training, or experience. Dr. Gardner's theory plays a significant role in rethinking how to educate so as to meet each student's individual needs. Basic skills can be more effectively acquired if all of a student's strengths are involved in the learning process.

The key to lesson design for a multiple intelligences learning environment is to reflect on the concept you want to teach and identify the intelligences that seem most appropriate for communicating the content. At Mountlake Terrace High School in Edmonds, Washington, Eeva Reeder's math students learn about algebraic equations kinesthetically by using the pavement in the school's yard like a giant graph. Using the large, square cement blocks of the pavement, they identify the axes, the X and Y coordinates, and plot themselves as points on the axes.

Other teachers will attempt to engage all eight intelligences in their lessons by using learning centers to focus on different approaches to the same concept. An example of this is Bruce Campbell's third grade classroom in Marysville, Washington. Campbell, a consultant on teaching through multiple intelligences, has designed a unit on Planet Earth that includes seven centers: a building center where students use clay to make models of the earth; a math center; a reading center; a music center where students study unit spelling words while listening to music; an art center using concentric circle patterns; a cooperative learning activity; a writing center titled "Things I would take with me on a journey to the center of the earth."

Another way to use the multiple intelligences theory in the classroom is through student projects. For example, Barbara Hoffman had her third-grade students in Country Day School in Costa Rica develop games in small groups. The students had to determine the objective and rules of the game. They researched questions and answers and designed and assembled a game board and accessories. Many intelligences were engaged through the creation of this project.

Dr. Gardner recommends that schools personalize their programs by providing apprenticeships. These should be designed to allow students to pursue their interests, with an emphasis on acquiring expertise over a period of time. In the Escuela Internacional Valle del Sol in Costa Rica, apprenticeships based on the eight intelligences are used. In one program long-term special subjects are offered to students in areas such as cooking, soccer, and drama. In addition, at the end of the term the entire school participates in a special project in multiage grouping with activities focused around a theme such as Egypt or European medieval life.

Assessment

The multiple intelligences theory challenges us to redefine assessment and see it as an integral part of the learning process. Dr. Gardner believes that many of the intelligences do not lend themselves to being measured by standardized paper and pencil tests. In a classroom structured on the multiple intelligences theory, assessment is integrated with learning and instruction and stimulates further learning. The teacher, the student, and his or her peers are involved in ongoing assessment. In this way the student has a better understanding of his or her strengths and weaknesses. Self-evaluation gives students the opportunity to set goals, to use higher-order thinking skills, as well as to generalize and personalize what they learn.

One example of nontraditional assessment is the development and maintenance of student portfolios, including drafts, sketches, and final products. Both student and teacher choose pieces that illustrate the student's growth. (Gardner calls these *process folios.*) Self-assessment can also include parental assessment, as well as watching videotaped student performances, and students editing or reviewing each other's work.

How to Use This Book

Multiple Intelligences: Teaching Kids the Way They Learn Grade 6 is designed to assist teachers in implementing this theory across the curriculum. This book is for teachers of students in sixth grade. It is divided into six subject areas: language arts, social studies, mathematics, science, fine arts, and physical education. Each subject area offers a collection of practical, creative ideas for teaching each of the eight intelligences. The book also offers reproducible student worksheets to supplement many of these activities. (A small image of the worksheet can be found next to the activity it supplements. Answers are provided at the end of the book.) Teachers may pick and choose from the various activities to develop a multiple intelligences program that meets their students' needs.

The activities are designed to help the teacher engage all the intelligences during the learning process so that the unique qualities of each student are recognized, encouraged, and cultivated. The activities provide opportunities for students to explore their individual interests and talents while learning the basic knowledge and skills that all must master. Each activity focuses on one intelligence; however, other intelligences will come into play since the intelligences naturally interact with each other.

As a teacher, you have the opportunity to provide a variety of educational experiences that can help students excel in their studies as well as discover new and exciting abilities and strengths within themselves. Your role in the learning process can provide students with an invaluable opportunity to fulfill their potential and enrich their lives.

Words of Advice

The following are some tips to assist you in using the Multiple Intelligences Theory in your classroom.

- Examine your own strengths and weaknesses in each of the intelligences. Call on others to help you expand your lessons to address the entire range of intelligences.

- Spend time in the early weeks of the school year working with your students to evaluate their comfort and proficiency within the various intelligences. Use your knowledge of their strengths to design and implement your teaching strategies.

- Refrain from "pigeonholing" your students into limited areas of intelligence. Realize that a student can grow from an activity that is not stressing his or her dominant intelligence.

- Work on goal-setting with students and help them develop plans to attain their goals.

- Develop a variety of assessment strategies and record-keeping tools.

- Flexibility is essential. The Multiple Intelligences Theory can be applied in a myriad of ways. There is no one right way.

The Eight Intelligences

Below is a brief definition of each of the eight intelligences, along with tips on how to recognize the characteristics of each and how to develop these intelligences in your students.

Verbal-Linguistic Intelligence

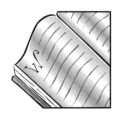

Verbal-linguistic intelligence consists of:

- a sensitivity to semantics—the meaning of words

- a sensitivity to syntax—the order among words

- a sensitivity to phonology—the sounds, rhythms, and inflections of words

- a sensitivity to the different functions of language, including its potential to excite, convince, stimulate, convey information, or please

Verbal-linguistic intelligence consists of the ability to think in words and to use words effectively, whether orally or in writing. The foundation of this intelligence is laid before birth, when the fetus develops hearing while still in the womb. It continues to develop after birth. Authors, poets, newscasters, journalists, public speakers, and playwrights are people who exhibit high degrees of linguistic intelligence.

People who are strongly linguistic like to read, write, tell stories or jokes, and play word games. They enjoy listening to stories or to people talking. They may have a good vocabulary or a good memory for names, places, dates, and trivia. They may spell words accurately and communicate to others effectively. They might also exhibit the ability to learn other languages.

Verbal-linguistic intelligence can be stimulated and developed in the classroom by providing a language rich environment. Classrooms in every subject area should include activities to help students develop a passion for language through speaking, hearing, reading, and examining words. Have students write stories, poems, jokes, letters, or journals. Provide opportunities for impromptu speaking, rapping, debate, storytelling, oral reading, silent reading, choral reading, and oral presentations. Involve students in class discussions and encourage them to ask questions and listen. Invite students to use storyboards, tape recorders, and word processors. Plan field trips to libraries, newspapers, or bookstores. Supply nontraditional materials such as comics and crossword puzzles to interest reluctant students.

Writing, listening, reading, and speaking effectively are key skills. The development of these four parts of linguistic intelligence can have a significant effect on a student's success in learning all subject areas and throughout life.

Logical-Mathematical Intelligence

Logical-mathematical intelligence consists of:

- the ability to use numbers effectively

- the ability to use inductive and deductive reasoning

- the ability to recognize abstract patterns

This intelligence encompasses three broad, interrelated fields: math, science, and logic. It begins when young children confront the physical objects of the world and ends with the understanding of abstract ideas. Throughout this process, a person develops a capacity to discern logical or numerical patterns and to handle long chains of reasoning. Scientists, mathematicians, computer programmers, bankers, accountants, and lawyers exhibit high degrees of logical-mathematical intelligence.

People with well-developed logical-mathematical intelligence like to find patterns and relationships among objects or numbers. They enjoy playing strategy games such as chess or checkers and solving riddles, logical puzzles, or brain teasers. They organize or categorize things and ask questions about how things work. These people easily solve math problems quickly in their heads. They may have a good sense of cause and effect and think on a more abstract or conceptual level.

Logical-mathematical intelligence can be stimulated and developed in the classroom by providing an environment in which students frequently experiment, classify, categorize, and analyze. Have students notice and work with numbers across the curriculum. Provide activities that focus on outlining, analogies, deciphering codes, or finding patterns and relationships.

Most adults use logical-mathematical intelligence in their daily lives to calculate household budgets, to make decisions, and to solve problems. Most professions depend in some way on this intelligence because it encompasses many kinds of thinking. The development of logical-mathematical intelligence benefits all aspects of life.

Bodily-Kinesthetic Intelligence

Bodily-kinesthetic intelligence consists of:

- the ability to control one's body movements to express ideas and feelings
- the capacity to handle objects skillfully, including the use of both fine and gross motor movements
- the ability to learn by movement, interaction, and participation

Bodily-kinesthetic intelligence begins with the control of automatic and voluntary movement and progresses to using the body in highly differentiated ways. The skillful manipulation of one's body or an object requires an acute sense of timing and direction, as well as the ability to transform an intention into action. Examples of people who possess bodily-kinesthetic intelligence are a dancer using his or her body as an object for expressive purposes and a basketball player who manipulates a ball with finesse. This intelligence can be seen in inventors, mechanics, actors, surgeons, swimmers, and artists.

People who are strongly bodily-kinesthetic enjoy working with their hands, have good coordination, and handle tools skillfully. They enjoy taking things apart and putting them back together. They prefer to manipulate objects to solve problems. They move, twitch, tap, or fidget while seated for a long time. They cleverly mimic other's gestures.

Many people find it difficult to understand and retain information that is taught only through their visual and auditory modes. They must manipulate or experience what they learn in order to understand and remember information. Bodily-kinesthetic individuals learn through doing and through multi-sensory experiences.

Bodily-kinesthetic intelligence can be stimulated and developed in the classroom through activities that involve physical movements such as role-playing, drama, mime, charades, dance, sports, and exercise. Have your students put on plays, puppet shows, or dance performances. Provide opportunities for students to manipulate and touch objects through activities such as painting, clay modeling, or building. Plan field trips to the theater, art museum, ballet, craft shows, and parks.

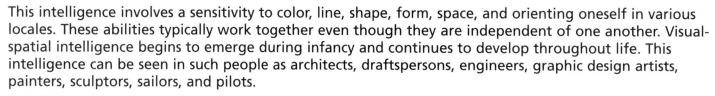

Visual-Spatial Intelligence

Visual-spatial intelligence consists of:

- the ability to perceive the visual-spatial world accurately
- the ability to think in pictures or visual imagery
- the ability to graphically represent visual or spatial ideas
- the ability to orient the body in space

This intelligence involves a sensitivity to color, line, shape, form, space, and orienting oneself in various locales. These abilities typically work together even though they are independent of one another. Visual-spatial intelligence begins to emerge during infancy and continues to develop throughout life. This intelligence can be seen in such people as architects, draftspersons, engineers, graphic design artists, painters, sculptors, sailors, and pilots.

Spatially skilled people enjoy art activities, jigsaw or visual perception puzzles, and mazes. They like to construct three-dimensional models. These people get more out of pictures than words in reading materials. They may excel at reading maps, charts, and diagrams. Also, they may have a good sense of direction.

Visual-spatial intelligence can be stimulated and developed in the classroom by providing a visually rich environment in which students frequently focus on images, pictures, and color. Provide opportunities for reading maps and charts, drawing diagrams and illustrations, constructing models, painting, coloring, and solving puzzles. Play games that require visual memory or spatial acuity. Use guided imagery, pretending, or active imagination exercises to have students solve problems. Use videos, slides, posters, charts, diagrams, telescopes, or color-coded material to teach the content area. Visit art museums, historical buildings, or planetariums.

Visual-spatial intelligence is an object-based intelligence. It functions in the concrete world, the world of objects and their locations. This intelligence underlies all human activity.

Musical Intelligence

Musical intelligence consists of:

- a sensitivity to pitch (melody), rhythm, and timbre (tone)
- an appreciation of musical expressiveness
- an ability to express oneself through music, rhythm, or dance

Dr. Gardner asserts that of all forms of intelligence, the consciousness-altering effect of musical intelligence is probably the greatest because of the impact of music on the state of the brain. He suggests that many individuals who have had frequent exposure to music can manipulate pitch, rhythm, and timbre to participate with some skill in composing, singing, or playing instruments. The early childhood years appear to be the most crucial period for musical growth. This intelligence can be seen in composers, conductors, instrumentalists, singers, and dancers.

Musically skilled people may remember the melodies of songs. They may have a good singing voice and tap rhythmically on a surface. Also, they may unconsciously hum to themselves and may be able to identify when musical notes are off-key. They enjoy singing songs, listening to music, playing an instrument, or attending musical performances.

Musical intelligence can be stimulated and developed in the classroom by providing opportunities to listen to musical recordings, to create and play musical instruments, or to sing and dance. Let students express their feelings or thoughts through using musical instruments, songs, or jingles. Play background music while the students are working. Plan field trips to the symphony, a recording studio, a musical, or an opera.

There are strong connections between music and emotions. By having music in the classroom, a positive emotional environment conducive to learning can be created. Lay the foundations of musical intelligence in your classroom by using music throughout the school day.

Interpersonal Intelligence

Interpersonal intelligence consists of:

- the ability to focus outward to other individuals
- the ability to sense other people's moods, temperaments, motivations, and intentions
- the ability to communicate, cooperate, and collaborate with others

In the early form of this intelligence, a young child possesses the ability to discriminate among the individuals around him or her and to detect their various moods. In the more advanced form of this intelligence, one can read the intentions and desires of other individuals and act upon that knowledge. This intelligence includes the ability to form and maintain relationships and to assume various roles within groups. The competence is prominent in political and religious leaders, salespeople, teachers, counselors, social workers, and therapists.

Interpersonally skilled people have the capacity to influence their peers and often excel at group work, team efforts, and collaborative projects. They enjoy social interaction and are sensitive to the feelings and moods of others. They tend to take leadership roles in activities with friends and often belong to clubs and other organizations.

Interpersonal intelligence can be developed and strengthened through maintaining a warm, accepting, supporting classroom environment. Provide opportunities for students to collaboratively work in groups. Have students peer teach and contribute to group discussions. Involve the students in situations where they have to be active listeners, be aware of other's feelings, motives, and opinions, and show empathy.

The positive development of interpersonal intelligence is an important step toward leading a successful and fulfilling life. Interpersonal intelligence is called upon in our daily lives as we interact with others in our communities, environments, nations, and world.

Intrapersonal Intelligence

Intrapersonal intelligence consists of:

- the ability to look inward to examine one's own thoughts and feelings
- the ability to control one's thoughts and emotions and consciously work with them
- the ability to express one's inner life
- the drive toward self-actualization

This intelligence focuses on the ability to develop a complete model of oneself, including one's desires, goals, anxieties, strengths, and limitations, and also to draw upon that model as a means of understanding and guiding one's behavior. In its basic form, it is the ability to distinguish a feeling of pleasure from one of pain, and to make a determination to either continue or withdraw from a situation based on this feeling. In the more advanced form of this intelligence, one has the ability to detect and to symbolize complex and highly differentiated sets of feelings. Some individuals with strong intrapersonal intelligence are philosophers, spiritual counselors, psychiatrists, and wise elders.

Intrapersonally skilled people are aware of their range of emotions and have a realistic sense of their strengths and weaknesses. They prefer to work independently and often have their own style of living and learning. They are able to accurately express their feelings and have a good sense of self-direction. They possess high self-confidence.

Intrapersonal intelligence can be developed through maintaining a warm, caring, nurturing environment that promotes self-esteem. Offer activities that require independent learning and imagination. During the school day, provide students with quiet time and private places to work and reflect. Provide long-term, meaningful learning projects that allow students to explore their interests and abilities. Encourage students to maintain portfolios and examine and make sense of their work. Involve students in activities that require them to explore their values, beliefs, and feelings.

Intrapersonal intelligence requires a lifetime of living and learning to inwardly know, be, and accept oneself. The classroom is a place where teachers can help students begin this journey of self-knowledge. Developing intrapersonal intelligence has far-reaching effects, since self-knowledge underlies success and fulfillment in life.

Naturalist Intelligence

Naturalist intelligence consists of:

- the ability to understand, appreciate, and enjoy the natural world
- the ability to observe, understand, and organize patterns in the natural environment
- the ability to nurture plants and animals

This intelligence focuses on the ability to recognize and classify the many different organic and inorganic species. Paleontologists, forest rangers, horticulturists, zoologists, and meteorologists exhibit naturalist intelligence.

People who exhibit strength in the naturalist intelligence are very much at home in nature. They enjoy being outdoors, camping, and hiking, as well as studying and learning about animals and plants. They can easily classify and identify various species.

Naturalist intelligence can be developed and strengthened through activities that involve hands-on labs, creating classroom habitats, caring for plants and animals, and classifying and discriminating species. Encourage your students to collect and classify seashells, insects, rocks, or other natural phenomena. Visit a museum of natural history, a university life sciences department, or nature center.

Naturalist intelligence enhances our lives. The more we know about the natural world, and the more we are able to recognize patterns in our environment, the better perspective we have on our role in natural cycles and our place in the universe.

REFERENCES

Armstrong, Thomas. *Multiple Intelligences in the Classroom*. Alexandria, VA: Assoc. for Supervision and Curriculum Development, 1994. A good overview of the Multiple Intelligences Theory and how to explore, introduce, and develop lessons on this theory.

Campbell, Linda, Bruce Campbell, and Dee Dickerson. *Teaching and Learning Through Multiple Intelligences*. Needham Heights, MA: Allyn and Bacon, 1996. An overview and resource of teaching strategies in musical, spatial, bodily-kinesthetic, interpersonal, and intrapersonal intelligences.

Gardner, Howard. *Frames of Mind: The Theory of Multiple Intelligences*. New York: Basic Books, 1993. A detailed analysis and explanation of the Multiple Intelligences Theory.

————. *Multiple Intelligences: The Theory in Practice*. New York: Basic Books, 1993. This book provides a coherent picture of what Gardner and his colleagues have learned about the educational applications of the Multiple Intelligences Theory over the last decade. It provides an overview of the theory and examines its implications for assessment and teaching from preschool to college admissions.

Haggerty, Brian A. *Nurturing Intelligences: A Guide to Multiple Intelligences Theory and Teaching*. Menlo Park, CA: Innovative Learning, Addison-Wesley, 1995. Principles, practical suggestions, and examples for applying the Multiple Intelligences Theory in the classroom. Exercises, problems, and puzzles introduce each of the seven intelligences.

Lazear, David. *Seven Pathways of Learning: Teaching Students and Parents About Multiple Intelligences*. Tucson: Zephyr Press, 1994. Assists in strengthening the child's personal intelligence and in integrating multiple intelligences into everyday life. Includes reproducibles and activities to involve parents.

————. *Seven Ways of Knowing: Teaching for Multiple Intelligences*. Arlington Heights, IL: IRI/SkyLight Training, 1992. A survey of the theory of multiple intelligences with many general activities for awakening and developing the intelligences.

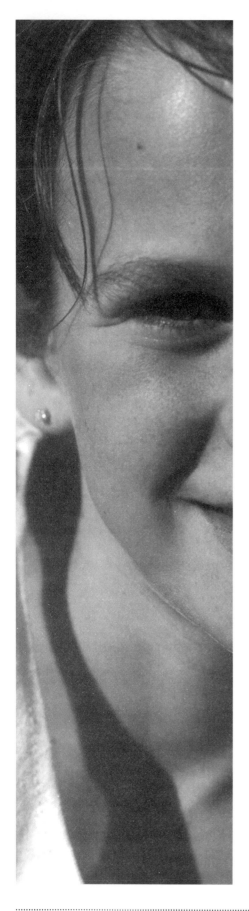

Verbal-Linguistic Intelligence

Need Some Advice?

Have students develop their linguistic intelligence by writing advice columns to literary characters. Choose some appropriate advice columns from newspapers and magazines to share with the students. Tell the students that they will ask for and give advice to literary characters. Ask the students to recall a book that the class has recently read in which the major character has had to solve a problem. An example might be Mary Lennox in Frances Hodgson Burnett's *The Secret Garden* (Grosset & Dunlap, 1996). Mary's problem is extreme loneliness and her need for friends and love. What if she could have asked advice from an advice columnist? What advice might the columnist have given Mary? Have each student select a character who has a problem from a book that the class is currently reading or has recently read. Have the students each write a letter to M. X. Pert, a fictitious advice columnist, asking for advice. Then have the students exchange their letters with a classmate. Tell the students that they are to play the role of M. X. Pert by writing back to the character to give advice. Let the students share the questions and responses with the class.

Cliché

In this activity students use their linguistic intelligence to focus on clichés. Explain that a cliché is a common phrase that expresses an idea. For example, "It's raining cats and dogs" means that it is raining very hard, or "in the doghouse" means that you are in trouble. Suggest that students become very conscious of clichés in their conversations and collect them over a set period of time. Tape a sheet of chart paper to the wall. Let the students write the clichés they hear. Some starters are "good as gold," "eat like a horse," "as sharp as a tack," and "as quiet as a mouse." When students have filled the chart, have them think of replacement expressions for these clichés. List these new expressions on the chart. Encourage students to use the winning expressions in their speech and writing.

Spelling Mnemonics

This activity helps students with their spelling by using mnemonics. Have students keep personal notebooks of the words they have difficulty spelling. Words may be from spelling lists or various assignments. Each week, have the students each choose several words from their notebook to learn how to spell. Have the student think up a mnemonic that helps him or her remember how to spell the words. For example, a student not sure of whether *i* or *e* comes first in *nieces,* might pair it with *nice,* in which *i* must always precede *e.* Thinking *nice nieces* will help the student spell the difficult word. A student having trouble remembering how to spell forty might develop the

mnemonic *It takes forty men to hold a fort.* At the end of each week, have students work in pairs to test each other on their words. Encourage students to reflect upon their work and evaluate their progress. They will be thrilled with their accomplishments!

While still in pairs have the students complete the **Anagrams** worksheet, on page 20. Have each student race the other in the pair to see who can complete the activity first.

Grammar Gaps

Here's a linguistic intelligence activity that will get students laughing while focusing on the parts of speech. In pencil, have each student write a short story or anecdote. Review the various parts of speech with the students. Then have the students remove ten words (parts of speech) from their stories and replace them with a blank. For example, they may remove nouns, pronouns, adjectives, verbs (past, present, or past participle), proper nouns, adverbs, conjunctions, prepositions, or interjections. Have the students label the blanks 1–10 and list the part of speech for each word they remove. Then put the students into pairs. Have the students ask their partner for an example of each part of speech on their list. For example, "Name one adjective. Name one preposition." (Be sure that students do not reveal the nature of their stories.) Have the students write the words in the blank. When all the blanks are filled, let the students read aloud their "revised" story. Students will chuckle at the hilarious results.

It's Debatable

Every argument has at least two sides, and sometimes more. Help students discover this concept through this linguistic intelligence activity. Plan and hold a debate on a subject that clearly has more than one point of view, such as whether television viewing time for children should be limited. Gauge the range of possible opinions. For example, some people would be firmly in favor of such limits. Others might accept limits only for the youngest children. Yet others may think there should not be any limits. Assign a debate team to argue each opinion. Suggest that each team develop at least three strong reasons for their argument. Have each group choose one person to present their three reasons. However, every member should be prepared to contribute to further discussion to answer questions or make comments. In staging the debate, encourage good speaking techniques, courtesy, and an adherence to time limits. Act as the moderator, setting a time limit on the presentation of each team's argument and allowing time for audience questions. Encourage audience members to prepare their questions in advance and to state which team a question is for.

Run-on Sentences

Show your students examples of run-on sentences and how to correct them before having them complete the **Stop the Run-ons** worksheet on page 21. A run-on sentence happens when two or more simple sentences are joined

page 20

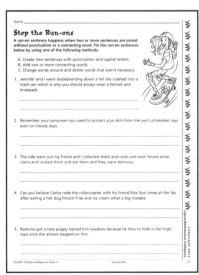

page 21

without punctuation or a connecting word. Here are some ways you can stop run-ons:

A. Create new sentences by using punctuation and capital letters.

B. Add a connecting word such as *and, but, so, while, as, when, because,* or *before.*

C. Change words around and get rid of words that aren't necessary.

Here is an example of a run-on sentence and a way to correct it:

Run-on sentence:

Dragonflies can move each pair of wings in a different direction this enables them to twist and turn, fly backward, hover, and dart up and down also.

Corrected sentence:

Because dragonflies can move each pair of wings in a different direction, they can twist and turn. They can also hover, fly backward, and dart up and down.

After your students have completed the worksheet, have them pair up and create and correct each other's run-on sentences.

Logical-Mathematical Intelligence

Finding Common Ground

Venn diagrams help the mathematical-intelligence student to analyze characters. Ask students to think of a fictional character they especially identify with and list his or her character traits. Then have the students make a list of their own character traits. Tell students to create a two-way Venn diagram for the character and themselves to examine what traits they do and do not share.

As Time Goes By

Develop logical-mathematical intelligence through this time line activity. After reading a story or chapter of a book, have the students create a time line. Divide the students into small groups. Give each group sentence strips and colored markers. Have each group analyze the story or chapter for the major events that took place. The groups write each major event on a sentence strip. Then the students arrange the strips in the order in which the events occurred. You may wish to have the groups exchange the sentence strips with one another and put the strips in order. The same technique can be applied to historical events and to ongoing stories in the news. To challenge students, use books or stories that have flashbacks.

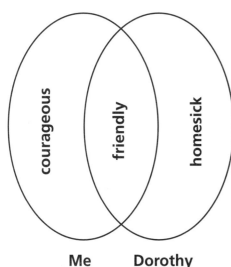

courageous friendly homesick

Me   **Dorothy**

Compare and Contrast Figures of Speech

Teach similes and metaphors using logical-mathematical intelligence. Many times poetry uses similes and metaphors. Explain to the students that a simile compares two unlike things using *like* or *as.* For example, *cheeks like roses* or *as big as an elephant.* Explain that a metaphor uses a word or phrase that ordinarily designates one kind of object or idea in place of another to suggest a likeness between them. For example, *the evening of life* or *drowning in money.* Give students various poetry books. Let the students search for similes and metaphors. List their findings on the board and discuss each. Then have the students write a simile and metaphor and illustrate each. Let students share their illustrations with the class, and have the class guess the comparisons.

Ups and Downs

Stimulate logical-mathematical intelligence with this character-graphing activity. Distribute graph paper to each student. Ask students to create a line graph that will record the chapter-by-chapter emotional highs and lows of a character in a book they are reading. Explain that the horizontal axis should represent the number of chapters in the book. They will have to determine what range of emotions the vertical axis should show. They might, for example, use a scale that shows a low at 0, a high at 5, and have 2 represent the middle range. If several students use the same novel, have them meet to compare their choices.

Context Clues Bookmarks

Stimulate logical-mathematical intelligence with this context clue activity. Give students 3" x 9" strips of paper, and have them make bookmarks. Have the students write the name of the book at the top of the bookmark. Then they should list any new words they encounter while reading. Beside each word, have them write the page number on which they discover the word. After the students are finished reading, ask them to look the words up in a dictionary and refer to the book for the original context. On a separate sheet of paper, have the students write the definition for each word without writing the word itself. Have students exchange books, bookmarks, and papers. Encourage students to look up the word in the book, read the word in the context of the sentence, and try to match the word with its proper definition.

Bodily-Kinesthetic Intelligence

Speaking in Signs

Expose children to a different kind of language—the manual alphabet used

Idea

by many hearing-impaired individuals. You may be able to find a volunteer who can demonstrate this to students. (Check in the yellow pages under Social and Human Services.) Or locate a chart of the manual alphabet in books such as *The Macmillan Visual Desk Reference* (Macmillan, 1993) or *A Show of Hands,* by Mary Beth Sullivan (Addison-Wesley, 1985). Teach children how to form the letters of the alphabet. Then practice finger spelling words.

Extend this activity by teaching signs that represent whole words. Point out that spoken language is based on an alphabet, just as sign language is. But alphabet letters are combined to form words that are spoken as single units, not spelled out letter by letter. Sign language works much the same way. Signs are combined and adapted to form whole words and phrases. Some simple examples to teach are the following:

Idea	Sign I at the forehead, then move hand away from face.
Elevator	Sign E about chest high and move hand up.
King	Sign K at the right shoulder; move diagonally across body.
Water	Form a W and tap it on the chin.

Old Sayings, New Truths

Let students use their bodily-kinesthetic intelligence to demonstrate the morals from various Aesop's fables. Discuss the following traditional morals with the students:

- A stitch in time saves nine.

- Haste makes waste.

- A fool and his (her) money are soon parted.

- Honesty is the best policy.

- Don't cry wolf.

- Don't count your chickens before they hatch.

- Some things are easier said than done.

- Slow and steady wins the race.

- Let well enough alone.

Place students into groups of three to five. Assign each group one of the sayings. Ask each team to create a short skit (of about five minutes duration) to act out a modern situation that supports the saying. For example, "Don't count your chickens before they hatch" might have a sports team planning a post-game celebration, only to lose because they are thinking more of the party than the game. Let each group perform their skit.

Visual-Spatial Intelligence

What's the Story?

This language activity encourages spatial intelligence. Collect a number of cartoon strips from daily or Sunday newspapers. Cut out the speech bubbles, and glue the pictures onto a blank piece of paper. Have the students work in pairs. Give each pair a cartoon strip and have them examine the pictures. Ask the students if it is instantly obvious what the story line is behind the drawings. Are the cartoon characters showing any particular emotion? If so, what? What kind of action is going on? What is the setting? What might have happened just before? What might happen afterward? Suggest that the students think of a story about these characters. Tell them to write their own dialogue for the characters in each picture. As an extension, give each pair two other sheets of paper. Have them draw and create a dialogue for a previous episode and for a follow-up episode. Encourage students to do rough drafts and spelling checks before they create their final versions.

Promoting Reading

This activity stimulates spatial intelligence. Collect a variety of magazines. Have the students examine the various advertisements. Suggest they think about which advertisements appeal to them, why the ad appeals to them, how color is used, what objects are used, what the ad is trying to sell, or the words, if any, that are used. Tell the students to pretend they work for an advertising firm. The firm has just been hired to create an advertisement to promote more reading and less television viewing. Give each student a 12" x 18" sheet of white construction paper. Explain that each student is to create an advertisement to promote reading. Suggest students think about the benefits of reading over watching television. Provide various supplies, such as colored paper, tissue paper, crayons, markers, chalk, paint, pastels, glue, or scissors. Let students share their advertisements with the class. Then display the advertisements in the hallways, library, and classrooms.

Musical Intelligence

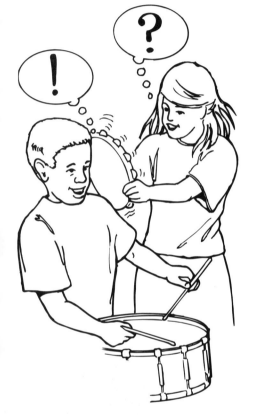

Musical Moments

Musical intelligence is used in this activity to focus on vocabulary. Give each student a 12" x 18" sheet of construction paper. Have the students divide the paper into six equal sections, and label the sections *sounds, actions, places, people, nature,* and *memories*. Select instrumental music that suggests visual and other sensory experiences, such as the opening of Handel's *Water Music*. Have students close their eyes and listen to the music several times through. Encourage students to think about images that describe the music. Then have the students translate the images the music creates into words that fit in the categories on their papers. Replay the music and have the students circle the words they feel are especially stirring and evocative of feelings and images. As a class, write a poem that suits the music. Encourage the students to use the words on their lists. Then have the students each write their own poem that suits the music using their word lists. Have the students share their poems as the music plays softly in the background.

Rhythmic Punctuation

Students can use musical intelligence to study punctuation marks. Gather a number of percussion instruments, such as small drums, cymbals, triangles, tambourines, and chimes. On the chalkboard, print all the punctuation marks that your students should be familiar with, such as period, question mark, exclamation point, comma, apostrophe, and quotation marks. Divide the students into several groups of "punctuation percussionists." Give each group the various percussion instruments. Have each group decide on which instrument should represent each form of punctuation. Point out that one instrument can represent more than one mark if it is played both loudly and softly. Have each group then select a narrator to read a paragraph from a book well known to the class. As the narrator reads, members of the group "punctuate" the reading by playing the proper instrument. Switch narrators so that each student gets a chance to be the narrator.

Musical Poetry

Enhance musical intelligence through this language arts activity. Have each student choose a favorite poem. Tell the students that their task will be to find an instrumental piece of music that will accompany their poem. Suggest that students focus on the rhythm of the poem to help them choose a musical piece with a similar rhythm. After students have found their musical selection, give them a week to practice reading their poems to the rhythm of their music. Encourage students to memorize their poems. Finally, have the students present their musical poetry to the class.

Interpersonal Intelligence

Meaningful Meetings

People often must work in groups to make meaningful decisions. This interpersonal activity helps students develop techniques to have a meaningful meeting. Divide the class into several groups. Give each group a topic to discuss and make a decision on, such as what play the class should perform for the school or what book the class should read next. Give no other guidelines. After ten minutes, bring the class together and ask students to evaluate their meetings. Use the following questions to stimulate discussion:

- Did your group have a natural leader or did you choose one?

- Did your group have a recorder to take down suggestions and decisions?

- Did everyone get a chance to speak? Did some people sit silently while others spoke frequently?

- Was the decision unanimous? Did everyone vote on it?

- Were you ready to tie up the discussion when time was called?

Open the discussion to suggestions for a set of guidelines for conducting a meeting. Suggestions may be: appoint a discussion leader, a recorder, and a timer; set a time limit for the meeting; ask the timer to give a three-minute warning before that time is up; and have the recorder summarize the decisions that were made. List the guidelines on a sheet of chart paper, and post them where they can be easily seen. Encourage students to use the guidelines in future group meetings. Students may wish to change or add to the guidelines after future meetings.

What's the Word?

This dynamic, interpersonal activity helps students develop their vocabulary. Pair your students with students from a lower grade level. Have your students share a short story or chapter book they have enjoyed reading. The younger students will probably find that some of the words may be too difficult for them. Have your students prepare a glossary of the difficult words in the story they are going to share with their lower grade level partners. Then arrange for a read-aloud time between partners. Have your students read the story aloud. Then leave it with the younger child after explaining how to use the glossary. At a later session, have the partners take turns reading the story to each other. Have your students share what they gained by the experience.

To Tell a Tale

Encourage interpersonal intelligence through this interactive language activity. Find a story, poem, or ballad with a good narrative that students can act out. One example is the traditional song "Arkansas Traveler" (found on *The Championship Years* by Mark O'Connor (Country Music Foundation, Nashville, TN 1990). Have the students retell the story. You may encourage students to use both choral and individual readings; acting and pantomime; and music. Divide the students into groups to develop costumes, sets, props, and cues. Choose students to be the directors. Rehearse and present the performance in class. Then invite other classes to see the performance.

Intrapersonal Intelligence

A Personal Viewpoint

Review with students the difference between first- and third-person writing using appropriate examples from their classroom reading. Next have them choose a passage from a book or story written in the third person. Encourage students to think about what the main character would know and feel about the situation being described. Then ask them to rewrite the selected passage in the first person, explaining what happened from the viewpoint of the character and describing what he or she thought, felt, and learned.

Are You Looking for Me?

Students will develop their intrapersonal intelligence through this language arts activity. Have the students bring in the employment sections from newspapers. Let students look at the various ads. Ask them if they see any positions they might like to hold someday. Have students read aloud some of the ads that appealed to them and explain why the ad grabbed their attention and interest. Tell students to use what they have read, as well as their own interests, to think about what the ideal job for them might be. Then have them write an ad for that ideal job. Finally, have them respond to the ad by writing a letter of application in which they list their interests, accomplishments (real or imaginary), and special qualifications for the position. Discuss with the students what they would expect to happen after submitting such a letter. Suppose they got a job interview. What kinds of questions might an interviewer ask? What would he or she expect in terms of the applicant's behavior? What responses and behaviors would cause an interviewer to reject an applicant? Students might role-play the roles of interviewer and interviewees, then analyze each mini-drama.

Reflecting on Learning Experiences

This intrapersonal activity encourages students to make sense out of their learning experiences in language arts and to articulate their thoughts. Each Friday, write an open-ended question about the week's language arts lesson(s) on the chalkboard. Have the students write an answer to the question by elaborating on what they learned. The question should only take the students a few minutes to answer. After the students finish writing, ask volunteers to share their answers. Have them read exactly what they wrote on their papers. This allows them to articulate their thinking. This activity may be adapted to other curriculum areas, such as science, social studies, or math.

Naturalist Intelligence

Biodiversity

Study biodiversity with your class by reading *Living Treasure: Saving Earth's Threatened Biodiversity,* by Laurence Pringle (Morrow, 1991). Other good resources are *Biodiversity,* by Dorothy Henshaw Patent (Clarion, 1996), and *Bats, Bugs, and Biodiversity: Adventures in the Amazonian Rain Forest,* by Susan Goodman (Atheneum, 1995).

Explain to your class that humans also exhibit the characteristics of biodiversity; some have freckles, some have red hair, some are green eyed, etc.

Create a biodiversity display in your classroom that can be developed throughout the year. Start by observing the human biodiversity in the classroom. Take photos of some students' hands, some students' eyes, others' smiles. Make sure all children are represented. Mount these photos for all to appreciate each person's individuality.

Add to the biodiversity display by having students collect any of the following: seashells, pine cones, leaves, bugs, nuts, feathers, and other objects from nature. Point out to students that there is diversity within each species as well as among them.

Sharp Senses

To give your students an opportunity to "stop and smell the roses" and put the experience into words, offer them copies of the **Sharp Senses** worksheet found on page 22. As a homework assignment, have them choose a spot outdoors for observation and record what they see, hear, touch, smell, and taste. (Point out that many observation opportunities will not involve taste, and that section may be blank.) Have students keep their completed forms and ask them to refer to them during the class's next creative writing exercise.

page 22

Anagrams

Rearrange the boldfaced word in each sentence to make a new word to complete each sentence.

1. "I will not use my **sword**," said the ruler, "but I will use _____."

2. The **lame** horse managed to limp to the barn in time to eat a _____.

3. The _____ made it to safety despite the **flow** of the river.

4. Finish peeling the potatoes and **stop** banging those _____.

5. Don't try to _____ by me like a silent **snake**.

6. Al tried to figure out which of the **two** cars he had to _____.

7. Michelle wasn't _____ her **ruse** would work.

8. Uncle Louie would tell you about **each** and every _____ he had.

9. Frank bragged that he didn't **own** anything he hadn't _____.

10. The path along the river was nothing but **miles** of _____.

11. Shirley was a **mite** tired after all the _____ she spent walking.

12. Looks like the runner may _____ the **sole** of his shoe.

13. Did you **ever** _____ off this path and go another way?

14. Julie held onto her friend's arm just _____ the **elbow**.

15. My mother has a _____ with facts about my whole **life**.

Stop the Run-ons

A run-on sentence happens when two or more sentences are joined without punctuation or a connecting word. Fix the run-on sentences below by using one of the following methods:

A. Create new sentences with punctuation and capital letters.
B. Add one or more connecting words.
C. Change words around and delete words that aren't necessary.

1. Jennifer and I went skateboarding down a hill she crashed into a trash can which is why you should always wear a helmet and kneepads.

   _____

   _____

2. Remember your sunscreen you need to protect your skin from the sun's ultraviolet rays even on cloudy days.

   _____

   _____

3. The tide went out my friend and I collected shells and rocks and even found some clams and cooked them and ate them and they were delicious.

   _____

   _____

4. Can you believe Carlos rode the rollercoaster with his friend Rita four times at the fair after eating a hot dog French Fries and ice cream what a big mistake.

   _____

   _____

5. Ramona got a new puppy named him sneakers because he likes to hide in her high-tops once she almost stepped on him.

   _____

   _____

Name _____

Sharp Senses

Successful writers are good observers who are always alert for new experiences. They use their senses as they react personally to these experiences. How does the snow sound underfoot? What does fresh-baked bread smell like? How does the surface of a warm woolen coat feel? These are all observations a writer might make and use later when describing something in a story.

Improve your observation powers by sharpening your senses. Go for a walk or find a quiet place to sit and observe. Then record everything your senses tell you about the experience. Write your observations in colorful detail so you will remember them. Don't just record that you heard the sound of water. Instead, describe the sound. Was the water rushing, trickling, or dripping? Later, use some of the observations in your own writing.

My observation experience: _____

Sights: _____

_____

_____

Sounds: _____

_____

_____

Textures: _____

_____

_____

Smells: _____

_____

_____

Tastes: _____

_____

_____

Verbal-Linguistic Intelligence

Civil War Articles

This activity helps students learn about the Civil War. Prior to the lesson, make a transparency of a current newspaper article. Show the students the article and have them read it. Have the students discuss the six story elements: Who? What? When? Where? How, and Why? Ask students if there are other details in the story and whether they are important. Have the students each write a news article on a Civil War event. Let the students research this era and choose a historical event on which to write, such as President Abraham Lincoln's speech at Gettysburg. (Have at least two students report on the same event.) Tell the students that they should write the news article as though they were there at the time. Remind them that their articles should answer the six story elements. Encourage students to add interesting details beyond the basic elements. Let the students share their articles with the class. Compare the stories and analyze the similarities and differences in the portrayals and perspectives they present.

Children in the Third World

As students study about third world countries, have them discuss the things that children in these countries do without every day. Ask them to brainstorm categories of basic need—such as food, water, shelter, and clothing—as you record their responses on a large sheet of chart paper. In each category, have students dictate the needs of children in the disadvantaged countries and the detrimental effects of being deprived of these necessities. Have students discuss the differences between wants and needs and how we view them in our country and in our personal lives. Ask each student to think about what they own and categorize it as either a want or a need.

Current Issues Debate

Debates are a super method to stimulate the students' linguistic intelligence while focusing on current issues. Place the students into groups of six. Assign each group a current issue that Congress or their state or city government will be voting on. Within the group, have three students work together and think of arguments for the issue, and have the other three students work together to think of arguments against the issue. Then have each group hold a debate. Set a time limit. Allow each side equal time to present each of their positions and for the other side to respond.

Trade Mission

This activity helps the student to learn about their state's economy. Explain to students that countries and states often try to generate foreign trade by welcoming trade missions from other countries. Divide the class into groups that will present different aspects of their state's economy, such as leading industries, major agricultural areas, and various services provided. Give each group a 9" x 12" sheet of construction paper and markers or paints. Ask each group to fold the paper widthwise into thirds. Have each group prepare a brochure that explains what goods are produced and which services are provided within their assigned state's economy. Provide encyclopedias and other reference materials for students to locate the information. Remind the students that the brochures should give reasons why the other countries should purchase these goods or services and also include illustrations. Have each group share their brochure with the class. Follow-up with a discussion on identifying and explaining the effects of various incentives to produce a good or service.

Logical-Mathematical Intelligence

Where Do You Want to Go?

Have students plan trips to different countries using a road map and the **Vacation Routes** worksheet on page 31. Students should pick a starting point and destination and write down the route. Then they should calculate the total miles traveled one way and the estimated time they would need to make the trip, allowing time for rest, meals, sleep, and refueling.

Comparing Ancient Civilizations

Stimulate students' logical-mathematical intelligence when teaching ancient civilizations. First, have the students brainstorm a list of attributes that describe two ancient civilizations, such as Mesopotamia and Egypt. Tell students that they are going to compare and contrast these two civilizations. On an overhead or chalkboard, draw a two-way Venn diagram. Label one circle Mesopotamia and the other circle Egypt. Then have the class complete the Venn diagram by listing the attributes in the appropriate sections. To challenge the students, draw a three-way Venn diagram to compare and contrast three ancient civilizations.

page 31

Bodily-Kinesthetic Intelligence

Famous Americans

Students will learn about famous Americans through this bodily-kinesthetic intelligence activity. Ask students to think of a historical figure they especially admire or whose example they would like to follow. It should be someone who has changed history in some way: an explorer whose discoveries changed the map of the world, a scientist who expanded knowledge, a doctor whose vaccine extended people's lives, a heroic figure who fought for freedom. Have students form groups and create a drama that acts out an important historical moment in the person's life. Some students can work on costume, others can work on dialogue, and others can be the actors.

Ancient Civilizations Game Board

This activity reviews ancient civilizations. Divide the students into groups of four. Reproduce the **Ancient Civilizations Game Board** on page 32 for each group. Give each group thirty 3" x 5" cards, four different buttons to use as game markers, and a die. Have the students write ancient civilization clues or questions on one side of the cards and the answers on the backside. For example, *What ancient civilization built pyramids?* or *Ancient Egypt developed in the* _____ . Then place the cards in a pile. To play, a student draws a card, reads the question, and answers the question. If the answer is correct, he or she rolls the die and moves his or her marker along the game board. The first person to get to the end wins. This game board can also be used to study each ancient civilization individually. Have students make question and answer cards for only one ancient civilization. Then play as stated above.

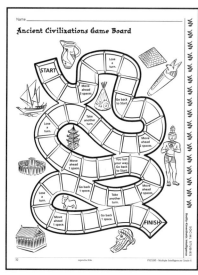

page 32

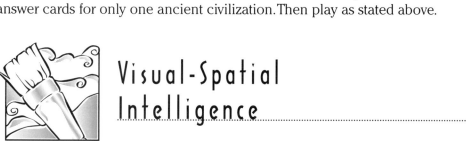

Visual-Spatial Intelligence

A Wall of Facts

Here's an activity to help students learn about China through spatial intelligence. Have the students recreate the Great Wall of China. Let students use 3" x 9" pieces of construction paper as the bricks for the wall. Have the students print an interesting fact about China on each brick and "construct" the wall on a bulletin board. As a variation, have students construct the wonders of other countries. For example, students can study Egypt by building a pyramid and France by constructing an Eiffel Tower.

Monumental Research

Stimulate spatial intelligence while learning about famous monuments. Show the students various pictures of famous monuments in the United States, such as the Jefferson Memorial, Washington Monument, Lincoln Memorial, Grant's Tomb, Vietnam Memorial, and Statue of Liberty. Display these on a bulletin board. Place the students into small groups. Have each group research one of these monuments to discover what the monument represents and other factual information about the monument. Have the groups write a paragraph about the monument and share their writings with the class. Then display each report next to the picture of the monument. Discuss the meaning these monuments have for us now. Follow-up by having each group design a monument that could represent their generation. Suggest that the monument be not only symbolic but also functional in a way that will actually enhance the lives of their generation and the generations that follow.

More Than Money

Have students identify the individuals that are honored on the money of this country or another country. Have students use reference sources to learn why these individuals were honored through coin or paper money. Have the students each design a coin or paper money for a person whom they believe should be honored today. Have them present their illustrations to the class and explain why this person should be honored.

Governmental Flow Chart

Flow charts are an excellent way to help students learn about the three branches of government. Use tagboard cards and markers to create a flow chart. First, as a class, identify the three branches of government—the executive, the legislative, and the judicial. Write each branch on a tagboard card using a different color marker for each. Display these in a pocket chart. Then write President, Congress, and Supreme Court each on a card using the color marker to match the governmental branch cards. Show the students each card, and let them place the card under the correct governmental branch card. Explain to the students that Congress is separated into the House of Representatives and the Senate. Write each on a card and place beneath the Congress card. As the students learn the duties and responsibilities of each branch, let them make additional cards and add them to the flow chart.

State Capital Fun

Here is a fun activity to help students identify the states and learn the state capitals. You will need a dart, an overhead marker, an overhead projector, and a transparency of the United States, without the states labeled. Project the map on an empty bulletin board. Have a student stand approximately six feet from the bulletin board and throw the dart. Ask the student to name the state that the dart hits, and then name the state capital. If the student is correct, let her or him write the state name and capital on the transparency. Then choose another student to throw the dart and try to hit a different state. Continue until all the states and capitals have been identified.

Musical Intelligence

Moving Along

Use a collection of traditional and other songs to help the musical intelligence student learn about different modes of transportation during various time periods. Choose a selection of traditional songs about transportation, such as "Shenandoah," "I've Been Working on the Railroad," "The Rock Island Line," or "The Erie Canal." Teach these and other, similar songs to the class. Encourage them to think of how workers might have used the rhythm of the music to help them work. What kinds of actions were the workers involved in as they worked? How does the rhythm of this song fit that action? Explain that songs have been written about most modes of traveling, including trucks, airplanes, and jet liners. Encourage students to share traveling songs from their musical experience. Suggest they adapt songs or write new ones about other modes of traveling, such as skateboards, in-line skates, or motor scooters.

You're on the Air

Tell your students that they have just been hired as disc jockeys at a local radio station. They will be given fifteen minutes to play three songs about issues that are personally important to them. Each song will get a short introduction that tells the listeners why the selection is chosen. Distribute the **Personal Program** worksheet on page 33 for students to use for this activity.

page 33

Interpersonal Intelligence

Where Am I?

Play the Where Am I? geography game when students are studying a particular continent, such as Asia. Display a map of the continent you are studying. Have each student choose a country within this continent and write a series of four clues about it. Divide the class into two teams—Team A and Team B. Have a member of Team A read a clue to a member of Team B. If the student answers correctly, the team scores as follows: on the first clue 8 points, on the second clue 4 points, on the third clue 2 points, and on the

---

Indonesia

Clue 1: This country is a chain of more than 13,600 islands.

Clue 2: About three-fifths of this country's population lives on one island.

Clue 3: This country produces rice, tea, and rubber.

Clue 4: It was once ruled by the Dutch.

fourth clue 1 point. Then have a member of Team B read a clue to a member of Team A. Continue playing until all the clues are used. Show the students the clues for Indonesia as an example.

What If

This interpersonal intelligence activity gets students to project their thoughts and ideas into an imaginary setting by changing historical events. Have the students work in pairs. Give the class a "what if" statement. For example, what if the South had won the Civil War? What if the Pilgrims had landed on the west coast? or What if Henry Ford had not invented the automobile? Have each pair reflect on how their lives and the country would be different. Have the pairs write down all the possible implications of the statement. Let the pairs share their thoughts with the class.

Travel Clubs

Encourage students who share an interest in visiting a specific country to form a travel club. Suggest that the students meet to discuss what they already know about the country. Then have them develop a list of things they would like to know more about. Have each club research the country, and develop an informational display, illustrating it with pictures of various sights. Invite a spokesperson from each club to give a guided "tour" of the wished-for destination. If possible, invite a travel agent or community member who has been to that area to share more information. Have the clubs go on an imaginary trip to the country they have studied. Tell them to keep a daily journey of the places they have visited and the experiences they have had during a week's visit. Or, suggest that they write one postcard or letter home for each day of their trip.

Story Circle

This interpersonal intelligence activity introduces students to the oral tradition of passing stories on. Students who have been to overnight camp may be able to share experiences of telling stories while sitting around a campfire. Tell students that oral storytelling is the way stories were passed on long before books or movies. Form storytelling teams and have each one choose a legend or traditional tale from various cultures to retell. The retellings should take about three to five minutes each. Suggest that each participant learn part of the story and be responsible for telling it. Encourage the teams to make their presentations realistic by using gestures and such props as costumes and a storytelling bag, from which they draw out props for their stories. As an extension, hold a storytelling festival and invite another class to form story circles. Have storytelling teams go from circle to circle to share their tales. Two sources for stories to retell are: *Realms of Gold: Myths and Legends From Around the World,* by Ann Pilling (Kingfisher, 1993), and *Keepers of the Earth,* by Michael J. Caduto (Fulcrum, 1988).

Intrapersonal Intelligence

Hoist the Flag

This intrapersonal intelligence activity helps students focus on the symbolism of world flags. Explain to the students that the symbols on the flags represent things about the country. Have the students examine the American flag. Ask the students what symbols and colors they see on the American flag. How many stars are there, and what do they represent? How many stripes are there, and what do they represent? Why are the colors red, white, and blue? Explain that the 13 stripes stand for the original colonies, and the 50 stars represent each state. By tradition, red symbolizes courage, white purity, and blue vigilance, perseverance, and justice.

Provide books and encyclopedias. Have students work in pairs to examine flags of other countries. Let students share what the symbols and colors represent. Then have the students create their own personal flags to represent themselves. Give each student drawing paper, construction paper, scissors, paints, markers, crayons, pencils and glue. Have students brainstorm a list of things about themselves that they would like to commemorate and symbols and colors that would represent these things. Suggest they make preliminary sketches. Finally, let the students share their flags with the class. Have them explain what the symbols and colors represent.

Economic Development

This intrapersonal activity helps students reflect on their understanding of the development of our economic system. Have students reflect on how individuals, such as John Deere, Thomas Edison, Henry McCormack, or Henry Ford contributed to economic change through ideas, inventions, and entrepreneurship. Have the students pretend that they are entrepreneurs. Ask them to develop a new idea or invention. Have students think about how their idea or invention will help the economy. Have students write about their idea or invention. Let those students who wish share their ideas or inventions with the class.

Being a Television Reporter

This intrapersonal activity allows students to review famous Americans. Have the students pretend they are television reporters and to think of a favorite famous American. Ask students to imagine interviewing this famous American. Have each student write a dialogue of the conversation.

Naturalist Intelligence

The Survival Game

Arrange students into groups of three and have members of each group count off from 1 to 3. Ask them to imagine the following scenario:

You are hikers traveling together in a wilderness area and you have become lost. It is late autumn—the nights are cold, but there hasn't yet been snow. The nearest town is at least a two-day walk, and there are no public roads until you reach that town. You are all wearing jeans, sweatshirts, heavy socks and hiking boots. In addition, each of you has the following:

Person 1	Person 2	Person 3
lighter	bag of raisins	jackknife
8-foot length of rope	ball of heavy twine	heavy wool blanket
compass	6 dried apples	pocket calculator
large plastic bag	mechanical pencil	several rubber bands

Have each group meet to discuss its survival plan. Using only what they have with them and what they can find in nature, how will they keep themselves warm, fed, and safe from predators? How will they find their way to safety? Then ask groups to share their plans with the rest of the class. Have them reflect on how they had to cooperate and whether any conflicts arose. Ask groups which items were most essential to their survival plan and whether any items were worthless to them.

Foreign Foods

When learning about different countries, students are often interested in the types of foods eaten by other people. Divide students into small groups and have each group choose a type of food from a selected country. Have students take note of how foods reflect natural resources and geography. For example, an island cuisine would naturally include seafood. Countries that rely heavily on dairy products would have a large amount of pastureland. After finding a desired recipe, have each group determine the ingredients needed and how they will obtain them. Allow students to prepare the recipe at home or in a school kitchen and share the treats with classmates on an International Food Day. Encourage students to explain how the cuisine reflects the resources and geography of the country.

Vacation Routes

Use an atlas to choose a starting point and
destination of your fantasy vacation in the
countries below. Write directions to get from one
place to the next. Calculate the total miles round
trip and the amount of days needed to take the vacation.

1. United States and Canada: From _____ to _____

    Total miles: _____ Estimated time: _____

    _____

    _____

2. South America: From _____ to _____

    Total miles: _____ Estimated time: _____

    _____

    _____

3. Western Europe: From _____ to _____

    Total miles: _____ Estimated time: _____

    _____

    _____

4. The Middle East: From _____ to _____

    Total miles: _____ Estimated time: _____

    _____

    _____

5. Asia: From _____ to _____

    Total miles: _____ Estimated time: _____

    _____

    _____

SOCIAL STUDIES Logical-Mathematical Intelligence

Name _____

Ancient Civilizations Game Board

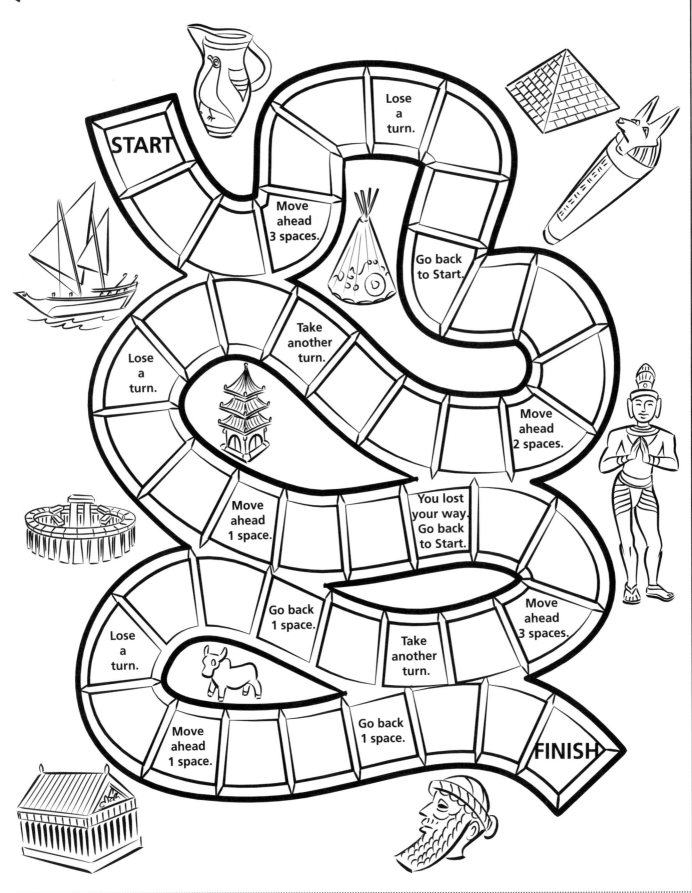

START

Lose a turn.

Move ahead 3 spaces.

Go back to Start.

Take another turn.

Lose a turn.

Move ahead 2 spaces.

Move ahead 1 space.

You lost your way. Go back to Start.

Move ahead 3 spaces.

Lose a turn.

Go back 1 space.

Take another turn.

Move ahead 1 space.

Go back 1 space.

FINISH

Name _____

Personal Program

The local radio station has just hired you to be a
disc jockey for 15 minutes. This is your chance to
play songs about issues that are important to you.
Select the music to play and write an introduction
for each selection, and an introduction and closing
to your program.

Program Introduction: _____

_____

_____

Selection 1: Title _____ Time: _____

Introduction: _____

_____

_____

Selection 2: Title _____ Time: _____

Introduction: _____

_____

_____

Selection 3: Title _____ Time: _____

Introduction: _____

_____

_____

Program Closing: _____

_____

_____

Try This! On the back of this paper, write a station promo for your show. Tell people what
to look forward to and when to tune in. The message should last 20 seconds.

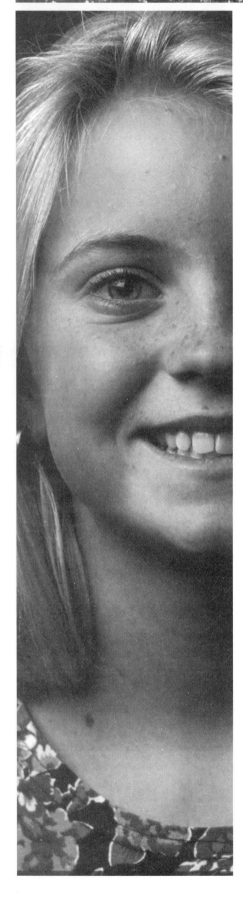

 # Verbal-Linguistic Intelligence

Break the Code

Ask the students to work in pairs for this activity. Each pair is to create a coded message using numbers in place of letters. Have the pairs follow these steps to make a code.

1. List the 26 letters of the alphabet.

2. Write a number problem beside each letter.

3. Solve these problems. (Each answer must have a different numerical value.)

4. Write out your message.

5. Replace each letter in the message with its corresponding number, which is the answer to the problem.

6. On a separate sheet of paper, write the 26 letters of the alphabet with each number problem beside it. (Don't write the answer to the problem.)

7. Write out your coded number message. (Don't use the letters.)

When the students are finished, have them exchange their coded message with another group. Then let the groups try to break the code. Explain that they must solve each number problem correctly and use these answers to try to break the code. Codes can be made using the operations the students may be learning or reviewing, such as multiplying decimals or adding fractions.

Prefixes: Mathematically Speaking

Knowing common math-related prefixes can help students understand the meanings of words. On the chalkboard, write each of the prefixes listed below.

(1) uni-	(4) quad-	(7) sept-	(100) centi-
(2) du- or bi-	(5) quint-	(8) octa- or octo-	
(3) tri-	(6) sex-	(10) dec-	

Invite students to use the meanings of the prefixes to help them answer questions you pose. Or write questions on index cards, with answers on the back, and display in the classroom as an independent activity. Sample questions are listed below.

· How many babies are in a set of sextuplets? Quintuplets? Triplets?

· How many musical notes are in an octave?

- In how many events would you compete in a decathlon? A triathlon? A biathlon?

- How many horns did triceratops have?

- How many years are in a century?

- How many legs does a quadruped have? A biped? An octopus?

- If a town is celebrating its centennial, how old is it?

- How many sides and angles are there in a triangle? A quadrilateral? An octagon? A decagon?

- How many people sing in a duet? A trio? An octet?

- If you're bilingual, how many languages do you speak? If you're trilingual?

- How many sets of three zeros are there in a billion? A septillion?

- If you work in a triad, how many people are in your group?

- How many years are in a decade?

- How many decades has an octogenarian lived?

- How many centimeters are in a meter?

Note to the teacher: Students may ask about a prefix for the number nine. Explain that the prefix *non-* can mean nine. However, it usually means *not*. If students are interested, some examples of *non-* as a number prefix are: nonagon (figure with 9 sides and angles) and nonet (nine voices or instruments).

Word Fractions

Have students complete the **Word Fractions** worksheet on page 44 to stimulate verbal-linguistic intelligence while they use their math skills. Then have them write their own word fraction problems and ask a classmate to solve them.

page 44

Logical-Mathematical Intelligence

What Are the Odds?

Show students the "official rules" of a sweepstakes offer or lottery ticket. Ask a student to locate the chances of winning, such as 1 in 1,000,000. Explain to the students that if one million people enter the contest, only one person wins. This is called the odds in favor of winning. Then ask the students, "If one person wins, how many people will lose?" Explain that 999,999 in 1,000,000 is the odds against winning. Explain that sweepstakes are held to encourage the public either to buy merchandise or make a contribution, and lotteries are specifically for raising money.

Give the students a problem and have them determine the odds in favor of and against winning. For example, their school is having a raffle to raise money for new science equipment. The school sold 500 tickets and Scott bought 20 tickets. What are Scott's odds in favor of and against winning? Call on students to answer. Then have the students write a problem, exchange their problems with a classmate, and solve the problem.

Gingerbread Cookie Fun

In this cooking activity students use their logical-mathematical skills to practice working with fractions. Prior to the lesson, write the cookie recipe at left on a transparency and place on an overhead projector.

Review the recipe with the students. Then tell the students to pretend that they have to make a triple batch of these cookies for the school bake sale. Have the students figure the amount of each ingredient and the number of cookies it will make. Review their answers. Then tell the students that a mother bought all of the cookies for her family. Ask the students, if there are four people in this family and each family member gets an equal amount of the cookies, how many cookies does each family member get? Now tell the students to pretend that they have to make a half batch of these cookies. Have the students figure the amount of each ingredient and the number of cookies it will make. Review their answers. Finally, tell the students that they have to make enough cookies so that each person in the class gets one cookie. Have the students figure out how many batches they will need to make and the amount of each ingredient. Then provide the ingredients and let the students make the cookies.

Flying the Friendly Skies

Stimulate logical-mathematical intelligence by having the students calculate flight times. For this activity, students will need an airline's listing of its major routes, which can be obtained either on the Web or by visiting a ticket office. You will also need a time-zone map, which can be found in an almanac. Have the students pretend they are going to be flying from one city to another city. Ask a student to choose two cities. Then have the students use the arrival and departure times from the airline's listing to figure out the time it takes to travel from one city to the next. Using a time-zone map, have students figure out if there is a time-zone change. Ask the students how this would affect the actual time it takes to travel from one city to the next. Ask whether they would gain or lose any time. If so, how many hours they would gain or lose? What is the actual time to travel?

Gingerbread Cookies

Makes 15 cookies

1/4 cup soft shortening

1/2 cup sugar

1/2 cup dark molasses

1/4 cup water

2 1/2 cups flour

3/4 teaspoon salt

1/2 teaspoon soda

3/4 teaspoon ginger

1/4 teaspoon nutmeg

1/8 teaspoon allspice

Bake 375 for 10–12 minutes

Let's Estimate

Encourage students' logical-mathematical intelligence through this estimation activity. Prior to the activity, have students cut out pictures and prices of clothing from various catalogs, and glue them on index cards. Place all of the cards in a department store shopping bag. Let students take turns drawing three cards from the shopping bag. (You may wish to have students draw more than three cards.) Have the student read the cost of each item out loud. Tell the class to mentally estimate the total cost. Have students share their estimates. Then have the students figure the actual total cost of the three items. Have students compare their estimates with the actual cost.

To encourage decision-making skills give each student a different shopping budget and then have them pick five cards. They should decide on what they want to buy and write a paragraph explaining their decision.

Probability Fun

Stimulate students' logical-mathematical intelligence with this probability activity. Give each student a lunch sack filled with 7 red cards, 4 blue cards, 3 yellow cards, 3 green cards, and 1 orange card. To make the cards, cut one-inch squares from construction paper. Tell the students the color and number of cards and list on the overhead. Then, write the following questions on the overhead: If you pull a card from the bag, what are your chances of getting a red card? a blue card? an orange card? Which cards would have equal chances? Explain that they are to guess which color card they will draw and write their guess down. Then draw a card and write down the color of the card they drew. Let students see how many times they guess correctly.

 # Bodily-Kinesthetic Intelligence

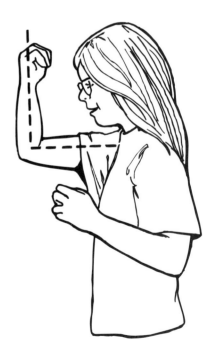

Body Angles

Have a quick review of angles, using arms instead of pencils. Ask students to stand far enough apart so they can stretch out their arms to the fullest. Then ask them to create a variety of angles using only their arms. For example, a right angle (90°) would be formed by holding the arm straight out from the shoulder and bent at the elbow with the hand pointing up. To form an obtuse angle (greater than 90°), the students would keep the upper arm steady and move the lower arm down. To form an acute angle (less than 90°), they would move the lower arm toward the shoulder. And a straight angle (180°) would be formed by stretching the arm straight out at shoulder height.

Hop to It

This small group activity provides practice adding and subtracting integers. Using chalk, draw a number line from –20 to +20 on the playground. You can also make the number line indoors using masking tape and number cards. Write or say an addition or subtraction integer problem, such as –5 + 2 = ___. Have the student start at 0 and then hop forward for each positive number and backward for each negative number to solve the problem. For example, the student would start at 0 and hop back five places (–5) and then hop forward two places (+2), ending up on –3 (the answer). As a variation and challenge, tell the students a word problem, such as Carla owed Craig $2. Carla earned $5 and paid Craig. How much money does Carla have? Have students use the number line to solve.

Viva Las Vegas

Have the students work in pairs in this activity, which reviews adding and subtracting integers. Give each pair two copies of the reproducible on page 45, **Integer Die,** a sheet of paper, and a pencil. (The worksheet should be photocopied onto heavy tagboard.) Ask the pairs to make the dice by writing positive and negative integers on the faces, and then taping the sides of each die. Have each student roll a die, and then use the two numbers to write either an addition or subtraction problem. Have the students solve the problem. Continue playing until the students have made and solved ten problems.

Statistically Speaking

This activity involves interpreting graphs. Tell the students that they will be creating a "living" bar graph. First, choose a topic for the bar graph that stimulates students' curiosity about themselves, such as favorite foods. Poll students to get their favorite food. Then, have each student who likes a particular food stand in one line. For example, all students whose favorite food is pizza stand in one line; those favoring hamburgers stand in another line parallel to the pizza students. Continue with the other favorite foods. Then, have students determine the longest line, the shortest line, and lines that are the same length. Pose questions about the graph, such as how many more students like pizza rather than hamburgers? Now, have the class determine the number of students in each category. List each category and number on the chalkboard. Have the students return to their seats.

Divide the students into three groups. Explain to the groups that each will use the information on the board to construct a different type of graph. Assign one group to create a bar graph, another group to create a circle graph, and the last group to create a picture graph. Tell the picture graph group that they will have to determine a common picture to use and determine the value of the picture, such as a happy face equals two people. Give each group a large sheet of construction paper, colored markers, and pencils to construct their graphs. When the groups are finished, display the three graphs. Have the students examine the three graphs, noting any similarities or differences. Then discuss with the students how the change of graphs can dramatically alter the visual message that is communicated.

page 45

Name _____

Integer Die

Cut out the die. Write positive and negative integers on its face. Fold and tape the sides together. Roll the die twice and use the two numbers to create an addition or subtraction problem.

Teacher: On heavy tagboard, reproduce two copies for each pair of students.

FS23285 · Multiple Intelligences Grade 6   reproducible   45

Visual-Spatial Intelligence

Class Flow Chart

Flow charts can be used while adding or subtracting fractions. Use sentence strips and colored markers to create a flow chart. First, as a class, identify the steps to solve an addition or subtraction fraction problem. Write each step on a separate sentence strip using a different colored marker. Cut the end of each sentence strip to look like an arrow. Once all the steps are written, arrange the strips sequentially along the edge of the chalkboard or display on a bulletin board. Now, give the class a problem to solve. Have the students read aloud each step and perform the step. Encourage students to use different colors for the numerators and denominators. Repeat with other problems. This technique can be used for other math computations, such as dividing two decimals or subtracting mixed numbers with renaming.

Subtracting Fractions

> Look at the denominators.

> Find the least common denominator.

> Write equivalent fractions using this denominator.

> Subtract the numerators. Write the difference over the common denominator.

Map It

This mapping activity activates the students' spatial intelligence to determine perimeter and area. Give each student a sheet of centimeter graph paper and colored markers. Have them each make a map of their bedrooms, classrooms, or neighborhoods by drawing different sizes of rectangles on the paper to represent each object or building. Encourage students to use different colored markers for each rectangle. Have the students measure and record the length of each side of the rectangles and determine the perimeters. Afterward, have the students use these lengths to find and record the area of each rectangle. Remind the students to record their answers in square units. Let the students examine their maps to determine what they notice about the perimeter and area of each rectangle. As a variation and challenge, have the students use different shapes, such as triangles, squares, and parallelograms.

Picture It

Here's an activity to help develop problem-solving skills. Before class, cut out pictures from magazines and newspapers that show some activity, such as people playing golf, animals running, or cars racing. Show the students one of these pictures. Let them examine the picture and write a story problem about the people, animals, or objects. Have the students solve the problem they write. Then have them exchange their problems with a classmate and solve their classmates' problem. Finally, have a few students share their problems and answers with the class. Repeat using other pictures.

Musical Intelligence

Notes

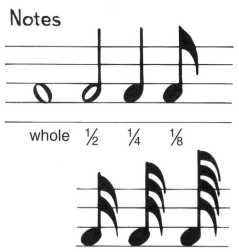

whole   ½   ¼   ⅛

¹⁄₁₆   ¹⁄₃₂   ¹⁄₆₄

Musical Beats

Musical beats and brainpower combine to make this a fun activity. Have students select a piece of music to listen to in class. Ask students to count the number of beats they hear in the first 15 seconds of the song. Then, based on the length of the song (this can usually be found on the jacket of the CD or cassette tape), have students calculate the total number of beats in the song. After students have tried this a few times, have them listen to a song and guess the number of beats before calculating.

Musical Fractions

Sheet music becomes interesting math work with this activity. Provide students with various pieces of sheet music. Discuss the time value of the notes on the page, such as whole notes, half notes, quarter notes, eighth notes, etc. Then have each student begin with the first line of music. The purpose of the activity is to add up the fractional values of the notes on the line and arrive at a total fractional value for that line. Students who are able to read music should act as tutors throughout the activity for those students who are not familiar with reading music. Children continue with each line of the music in the same manner. When students have completed a page of music, have them work with partners to check each other's work. Hint: You may want to begin the activity with very simple pieces of music and move to more difficult pieces as students are ready for a greater challenge.

Interpersonal Intelligence

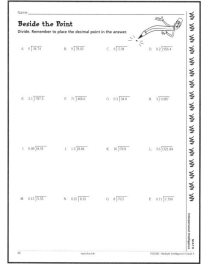

page 46

Encouragement

Make practice and drill worksheets exciting while promoting interpersonal intelligence. Place the students into groups of five and give each person the **Beside the Point** worksheet on page 46. Tell the students their goal for today is for every group member to know how to solve all of the problems on the worksheet. Have the students within each group divide the problems among themselves equally. Tell the students that each group member will take turns to solve problems out loud. The other students check for accuracy and suggest changes in solving the problem. Remind the students to encourage each other's efforts. Continue using this format until each group solves all the problems and believes that they met their goal.

Peer Tutors

Most students find that their math skills are stronger in certain areas than in others. Give your students the chance to learn from one another and assist their peers as well. Display a sign-up sheet on a wall in your classroom. Have students list the math skills with which they feel confident enough to tutor others. Encourage all students to evaluate their own math skills and determine areas where they might benefit from some extra assistance. Urge students to seek out peer tutors when needed to receive math assistance.

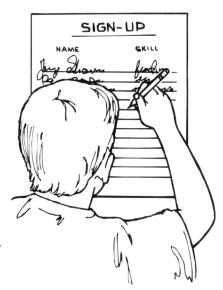

Cooperative Problem Solving

Divide your students into groups of four. Assign each student a role to play, based on the role descriptions below. Then present students with a word problem dealing with a chosen skill. Students should work together to arrive at a solution. When the group problem-solving process is complete, have students share their feelings about working with the group and acting in their roles.

Reader/Announcer—This student reads the question to the group and also explains the group's problem-solving process to the whole class after solving.

Writer—This student uses paper and pencil to record the group's calculations.

Questioner—This student is responsible for questioning the group's strategies throughout the problem-solving process. The questioner might ask questions such as, "What information do we need to know in order to solve the problem?" or "What materials should we use to solve it?" and "Should we figure out a way to check our answer?"

Encourager—This student's job is to keep the group working by providing positive feedback for each student's participation. This student should complement useful suggestions made by others and also praise the whole group by making encouraging comments such as, "We're doing great! Let's keep working."

Intrapersonal Intelligence

Real Life Word Problems

Encourage students to create word problems based on actual events in their lives. For example:

Sharon has saved up $70.00 for a CD player. Her mother promised to give her $30.00 for her birthday to use for the CD player. If the CD player costs $150.00, what percentage of the total price does Sharon already have?

Encourage the students to use fractions, decimals, ratio, and negative integers in their problems.

Math Journals

Have each student keep a math journal. Provide five minutes at the end of each math lesson for students to write in their journals. They may write what they learned in math, what they would like to learn, their mathematical strengths or weaknesses, what they did not understand, what they would like to improve upon, a problem they liked, a problem they had difficulty answering, or their own math problems. Also, encourage students to compile samples of their work in the journal and review them periodically. Discuss setting goals with them and monitor their progress in meeting their goals.

A Personal Graph

This graphing activity encourages students to use their intrapersonal intelligence. Have the students create a line graph of their feelings about math class for a week. On Monday, explain to the students that at the end of each math lesson, they are to reflect and explore their feelings about the math lesson. Give each student a line graph. Explain that the scale is from 1 to 10 with 1 being the worst feeling and 10 being the best feeling. Suggest that the students write a sentence about why they felt the way they did. Ask the students to write the name of the weekday next to the sentence.

 Naturalist Intelligence

Nature's Geometry Scavenger Hunt

Arrange students into pairs or small groups and send them outside on a Geometry Scavenger Hunt. Set the boundaries of the search area according to your circumstances: the outside play area, a park (or make it a homework assignment for students to complete in their neighborhood). Then provide each group with a list of items to be found. Suggestions are included at the end of this activity. Vary your list according to terms taught and items available in the search area.

Explain that groups must stay together as they search. They should check off any items they find, and for each they must record where the item was spotted. These records must be specific. For example, it isn't enough to say that an acute angle was spotted on a tree. The explanation should say what kind of tree and where it was located.

Set a time limit for the search. When the time is up, gather the groups together and see how many items were found by each group. Spot-check accuracy by asking each group to share what they wrote about several of

their finds. If some of the items could not be found, discuss where the shapes and angles could possibly be located in nature. For example, a cone could be found in a shell; a spiral could be found in a galaxy. What other shapes can the students find that are not on the list? (A heart, a tear drop, a diamond, etc.) Be sure to examine unfamiliar objects such as butterfly wings, microsopic photographs of nature, outer space, dinosaurs, fish, etc.

Search for...

circle	right angle	cylinder
square	acute angle	horizontal line
rectangle	obtuse angle	vertical line
hexagon	semicircle	polygon with 2 acute angles
spiral	star	cone
octagon	oval	cube
triangle	set of parallel lines	
set of perpendicular lines		

Weather Patterns

Have students keep track of the weather over a period of at least three weeks. Collect data about precipitation, extent and type of cloud cover, high and low temperatures, and wind speed and direction. Data can be a combination of observation, measurement, and use of published or broadcast weather reports. Keep track of the information on a class-sized weather chart. At the end of the time period, have students study the data they collected to see if there are any patterns revealed. Did the air temperature seem to be affected by precipitation or the amount of cloud cover? Were specific cloud formations associated with specific weather phenomenon? Did wind direction appear to have anything to do with precipitation? Discuss the students' observations.

Name _____

Word Fractions

Solve each word puzzle.

A. 3/5 of SHAPE is a kind of primate. _____ape_____

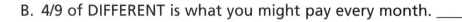

B. 4/9 of DIFFERENT is what you might pay every month. _____

C. 4/7 of DIAGRAM is a kind of metric measure. _____

D. 1/2 of TIME is the opposite of YOU. _____

E. 3/7 of COUNTRY is what you do all the time on your work. _____

F. 3/4 of FEEL can be very slippery. _____

G. 2/3 of PLANES is what you must stay in on a highway. _____

H. 7/9 of FRACTIONS speak louder than words. _____

I. 4/7 of NUMBERS is without feeling. _____

J. 4/5 of SEVEN is what 2, 4, 66, and 100 are. _____

K. 4/9 of CHALLENGE is a large room. _____

L. 1/3 of MANUFACTURER is something you can check. _____

Try This! Write your own word fractions. Have a classmate try to solve each puzzle.

_____

_____

_____

Integer Die

Cut out the die. Write positive and negative integers on its face. Fold and tape the sides together. Roll the die twice and use the two numbers to create an addition or subtraction problem.

Teacher: On heavy tagboard, reproduce two copies for each pair of students.

Beside the Point

Divide. Remember to place the decimal point in the answer.

A. $6\overline{)34.74}$

B. $9\overline{)78.03}$

C. $6\overline{)5.94}$

D. $0.2\overline{)956.4}$

E. $2.1\overline{)787.5}$

F. $71\overline{)468.6}$

G. $0.3\overline{)34.8}$

H. $3\overline{)0.987}$

I. $0.09\overline{)8.91}$

J. $1.3\overline{)8.84}$

K. $16\overline{)76.8}$

L. $3.6\overline{)321.84}$

M. $0.15\overline{)5.55}$

N. $0.25\overline{)8.33}$

O. $8\overline{)70.5}$

P. $0.71\overline{)1.704}$

Verbal-Linguistic Intelligence

Weather Poems

Here is a closing, linguistic intelligence activity to do with your class when you have finished studying weather. Have the students brainstorm a list of words or phrases about weather. List their suggestions on the chalkboard. Then have each student write a poem about weather. Students may wish to choose one type of precipitation or weather concept to write about, such as rain or wind. Encourage students to use the words or phrases on the chalkboard. Let students share their poems with the class.

Extinct Is Forever

Here's an intrapersonal intelligence activity for your unit on endangered animals. First, write the word *extinct* on the chalkboard, and have the students brainstorm a list of words that relate to this word. Write the list on the board. Then have the students think about and express their feelings of animals becoming extinct. Discuss which animals are on the endangered species list. Ask each student to choose an endangered animal that they are interested in learning how to help protect and research the animal. (The Internet provides several Web sites involved with protecting endangered animals.) Then have each student write a persuasive letter asking the public to support measures that would further protect this endangered animal. Encourage students to include specific information, such as the animal's habitat and range, present numbers, why the animal is endangered, what is being done to protect the animal, and other ways to protect the animal. Finally, let the students share their letters with the class.

Science Analogies

Review the use of analogies with students. Write the following example on the chalkboard: A tennis ball goes with a racket in the same way that a baseball goes with a _____. Ask students if they can fill in the missing word *(bat)*. Discuss how they determined the answer. Help them understand that to solve the problem they need to identify the relationship of the first two terms (a tennis ball is used with or hit by a racket) and then think of a word that goes with baseball in the same way.

Show students how the sentence below would be written as an analogy:

tennis ball : racket as baseball : bat

Point out that identifying the relationships within an analogy means knowing something about the terms being used. Explain that they can use what they know about science to solve the following analogy:

water : liquid as oxygen : _____

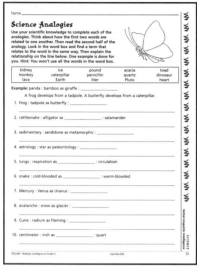

page 55

page 56

Ask them to identify the relationship between the first two words. (Water is an example of a liquid.) Then have them identify the missing word and explain how the relationship between the first two words helped them determine the answer. (What is oxygen an example of? A gas.) Provide students with copies of the **Science Analogies** worksheet found on page 55. Have them complete the analogies and explain their thinking in determining the answers.

Eponyms

An eponym is a real or fictitious person whose name is used to name a country, an institution, an invention, or other thing. William Penn, for example, is the eponym of Pennsylvania. Rome was named for Romulus. Many scientific discoveries are named for the people who discovered or researched them. Distribute the **Eponyms** worksheet on page 56 to the class and have them research the scientists.

Logical-Mathematical Intelligence

Comparison Charts

Divide the students into groups of four. Assign each group a different family of animals to research, such as canines or felines. Have the groups research several animals in their family. For example, the feline family group may research a lion, tiger, mountain lion, bobcat, lynx, jaguar, snow leopard, and domestic cat. Then have the groups each make a chart comparing the animals' characteristics, such as size, shape, color, food, offspring, and habitat. Each group can present their charts to the class.

Make a Sundial

Use this activity during your unit about the sun. Explain to the students that there are two parts to a sundial—the dial face and the gnomon, which casts the shadow. Have the class create a sundial. You will need a clay flowerpot that has a hole on the bottom, a dowel with a diameter slightly smaller than the hole on the bottom of the flowerpot and that is twice the height of the flowerpot, and a piece of chalk. To create the sundial, follow the steps below:

1. Set the flowerpot upside down on the playground in a sunny place. Push the dowel through the hole.

2. Every hour on the hour, use the chalk to make a mark where the gnomon casts its shadow. (Have the students mark the sundial for at least four consecutive hours.)

3. Tell the students to figure out where the other hours are by measuring equal distances around the dial.

Bodily-Kinesthetic Intelligence

Continental Drift

Students can use their bodily-kinesthetic intelligence to learn that the continents are moving. Explain to the class that the continents move on huge pieces of rock called plates. Scientists believe that millions of years ago there was a single continent called Pangaea and that over the centuries it continued to shift and break apart, eventually producing the configuration we have today. Show the students world maps of the land configurations from 200, 150, 100, and 50 million years ago. Discuss the gradual movements and configurations of the plates. Then divide the students into groups of seven. Have each student be one of the seven continents. Let them make cut outs of each continent and label appropriately. Have each group create a dance-pantomime that shows the gradual changes. The dance ends when all the continents are in their present-day relationship to one another. Suggest that students find music that is slow and mysterious to use for background. And as a follow-up, ask students to create their own hypotheses about where the continents, which continue to move, will be 50 million years from now and what changes that will bring.

Pangaea

Make a Fossil

Students can make a leaf or feather fossil with a plaster of paris cast. Each student will need a small pie tin, a leaf or feather, petroleum jelly, plaster of paris, a plastic spoon, a bowl, soap, and warm water. Follow the instructions to make the imprint.

1. Cover the sides and bottom of the pie tin with a thin layer of petroleum jelly.

2. Cover the leaf or feather with petroleum jelly and place it on the bottom of the pie tin.

3. Prepare the plaster of paris according to the directions, making a thick, smooth mixture. Pour it slowly over the leaf or feather until about a one-half inch layer covers the bottom of the tin.

4. Let it dry for about 30 minutes.

5. Carefully remove the plaster cast, and use warm water and soap to wash off the petroleum jelly.

6. Let the plaster cast dry overnight.

Explain that this is one way in which fossils are formed; that is, animal and plant remains are buried in sediment and then completely washed away, producing an imprint.

Visual-Spatial Intelligence

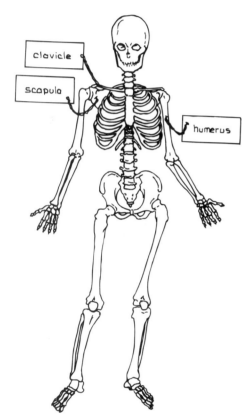

clavicle

scapula

humerus

The Skeletal System

Here's an interactive bulletin board to help students study the human skeleton. Display a large picture of the human skeleton on a bulletin board. Write the name of each bone on index cards. Randomly display these cards around the picture. Tape a length of yarn to each card. Have the student match the word card to the correct skeletal part by attaching the end of the yarn to the correct skeletal part with a push pin. Provide an answer key for the student to check his or her answers. This idea can also be used when studying the digestive system or muscular system.

Rocks and Minerals

As a wrap-up to your rocks and minerals unit, brainstorm a list of words students learned during the unit, such as *igneous rock, shale,* or *olivine.* Have each student choose 8–12 of these words and write a sentence for each word. For example: *Shale is clay or mud that became sedimentary rock. Igneous rock is formed from molten material in or below the earth's crust. Olivine is the most abundant mineral of the earth's upper mantle.* Then ask them to copy these sentences on another piece of paper but put a blank line in place of the vocabulary word. Next give each student two sheets of centimeter graph paper. Have each student create a word-find puzzle for these words on one sheet. Then copy the word-find puzzle on the second sheet and circle the answers to create an answer sheet. Staple the sentence and word-find puzzle papers together. Then have the students switch papers with a classmate. Let the students read their classmates' sentences and solve the word-find puzzle.

Food Chain Mobiles

Explain to the students that a food chain is the relationship between all living and nonliving things, especially the movement of food and energy through an ecosystem. To create food chain mobiles, give each of the students old magazines, construction paper, yarn, scissors, and glue or tape. Have the students each choose an environment, such as the woods. Let each student cut out or draw pictures to create a food chain from this environment. For example, a sun, some plants, a rabbit, an owl. Tell the students to glue the pictures to the construction paper and cut again, leaving a small border around each picture. Then cut a length of yarn and attach the pictures in chronological order. Let each student explain their food chain to another classmate. Hang the mobiles in the classroom.

Musical Intelligence

Extreme Weather Songs

Let students use their musical intelligence to review extreme weather conditions. Divide the students into groups of five. Have each group write a song or rap that expresses some of their knowledge about different kinds of extreme weather. Encourage students first to brainstorm a list of words or phrases of their knowledge and think of words that rhyme with them. Then they can use this list to assist them in their writing. Let each group perform their song or rap for the class. Provide percussion instruments to be used during the performance.

Setting Nature to Music

Invite students to listen to and enjoy classical music with nature themes. Identify the name and composer of the piece. Then play a short selection from the larger work. Provide time for students to give their reactions, asking them to consider how the composer used music to represent nature. Were there passages that sounded like water or waves? Like wind or rain? Some appropriate compositions include:

· *La Mer,* by Claude Debussy

· *The Four Seasons,* by Antonio Vivaldi

· *Grand Canyon Suite,* by Ferde Grofé

· *The Water Music,* by George F. Handel

Interpersonal Intelligence

What a Race!

Here's an interpersonal intelligence game for students to review their knowledge about matter. Prior to the game, divide the students into pairs. Give each pair five index cards. Have each pair write a matter question on one side of each card and the answer on the backside. For example, *What is*

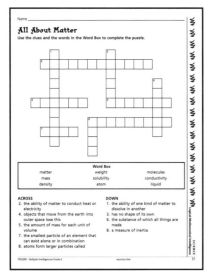

page 57

matter? (anything that occupies space) or *What are the three particles all atoms are made of?* (electrons, protons, neutrons). Collect the cards. Also, draw, cut out, and laminate four race cars from different colored construction paper. Then draw a long, curvy race track with four lanes on the chalkboard. Divide the race track into approximately twenty sections; label the first section of each lane *Start* and the last section of each lane *Finish.* Divide the class into four groups. Assign each group a car, and tape each car to a lane at the Start section. Have each group choose a spokesperson for the team. To play, ask each group a question in rotation. The group discusses the question, decides on an answer, and their team spokesperson gives their answer. If the group responds correctly, move their car forward 1 space. The first car to reach the Finish section is the winner. This game can be played using other science topics that are covered throughout the school year.

As an extension to this activity, distribute the **All About Matter** worksheet on page 57 for the class to complete.

How It Works

Develop students' interpersonal intelligence through this peer teaching activity. Suggest that students each research a common device that is frequently used but not necessarily understood by most people. Examples might include a telephone, a camera, a remote control, a refrigerator, or a microwave oven. Ask students to find out how the device works and to be able to explain the procedure to a classmate. Encourage students to use diagrams and other visuals when they give their explanations. Divide the students into groups of three. Have each student teach their peers about how their device works.

Shadows

In this activity students use their interpersonal intelligence to study shadows. Have the students work in pairs. Give each pair a yardstick, compass, pencil, and writing paper. Have the students go outside at the beginning of the school day, at noon, and at the end of the school day. Ask students to stand with their backs to the sun; to observe, measure, and record the lengths of their shadows; and to determine and record the direction in which their shadows are pointing. Then have the students examine and discuss their results. Stimulate the discussion by asking questions such as, *Did the position and lengths of shadow change? If so, how? Could you determine the time of day by the lengths of your shadow? Could you determine the direction you are walking by your shadow? How or when might this information be helpful?*

Intrapersonal Intelligence

What I Learned in Science

Here's an intrapersonal intelligence activity that gets students to reflect upon the progress they are making. Have the students use a spiral notebook to make a science journal. After each science unit, weekly or daily lesson, or science experiment, have each student write about what they knew and what they learned about the science topic. Ask students to review their journal entries periodically. By the end of the year, students will have a book of their entire science learning experience!

Taste Experiments

We use our tongues to taste things that are sweet, salty, sour, and bitter. Do you know which part of the tongue can taste each of these? Sweet is tasted at the front of the tongue. Salt is tasted on the sides near the tip of the tongue. Sour is tasted along the side, and bitter at the back of the tongue.

Have students draw a diagram of the tongue and do the experiment below. As they complete the activity they should label their drawing of the tongue sweet, salty, sour, and bitter in the appropriate areas.

Provide students with several cotton swabs and three small cups filled with the following substances:

- sweet—sugar water
- salty—salt water
- sour—lemon juice
- bitter—strong coffee unsweetened

Students should be instructed to dip a cotton swab into a substance and then run it over different areas of the tongue to identify where it can be tasted. After testing each substance, have students mark their tongue drawing.

To extend the activity, explain to students that when they hold their noses they cut off the flow of air to their olfactory receptors (smelling sensors) inside the nose. This will dull their sense of taste. Tell students to work in pairs to test their dulled senses. Give each pair of students two slices of orange and two slices of grapefruit. Then challenge them to close their eyes and hold their nose while their partner feeds them a piece of fruit with a fork. They have to try to guess which piece of fruit is which. After all students have tried the experiment, discuss the results with the class.

Naturalist Intelligence

A Nature Hunt

Here's a naturalist intelligence activity to use in conjunction with your plant unit. Students will use their naturalist intelligence to go on a nature hunt. Make a list of several items for each student to find, and reproduce the list for each student. For example: find three kinds of trees, find five kinds of petals, find three kinds of seeds, find three plants with different colors, and find two vascular plants. Have each student take a piece of drawing paper and pencil with them on the nature hunt. Take the students outside or to the park, if possible. Let the students find each item on the list and make a sketch of each item they find. Afterward, have the students share their results with the class and compile this information to make a large chart. Students will be amazed by the variety of results!

Natural Movements

Observing animals and plants in their natural habitats encourages development of the naturalist intelligence. During the spring, take the students on a field trip to a park. Have the students take a hike through the woods. Let the students observe the movements of various animals and plants, such as ants, deer, birds, butterflies, trees, or flowers. Discuss any similarities or differences in these movements. Then discuss how the students might move their bodies to pantomime these movements. Call out an animal or plant they observed and have the students move their bodies to pantomime these movements. Let small groups of students develop a three-minute dance program based on the movements they observed. For example, a group might pantomime a tree blowing in the wind that starts out as a light breeze, then becomes very strong, and finally dies down; worker ants carrying food back to their nest; baby birds trying their wings; bees gathering pollen; or a snake slithering through the brush. Play "nature" music as the students practice and give their performances.

Bird Watching

Develop students' naturalist intelligence by having the class observe birds throughout the school year. Have the class build several different types of bird feeders. If possible, place these feeders in a place where they can be viewed from a window in the classroom. On a regular basis, have the students observe the kinds of birds that visit each feeder. Have students keep a journal of the names of the birds, which feeder the birds visited, and the when they were observed (time and day). If the students don't know the bird's name, have them draw and color a picture of the bird. Then provide reference books for the students to identify the bird. Have students use this information to make graphs showing how frequently a particular bird was observed.

Name _____

Science Analogies

Use your scientific knowledge to complete each of the analogies. Think about how the first two words are related to one another. Then read the second half of the analogy. Look in the word box and find a term that relates to the word in the same way. Then explain the relationship on the line below. One example is done for you. Hint: You won't use all the words in the word box.

kidney	ice	pound	acacia	toad
monkey	caterpillar	penicillin	quartz	dinosaur
lava	Earth	liter	Pluto	heart

Example: panda : bamboo as giraffe : _____

A panda eats bamboo. A giraffe eats acacia.

1. frog : tadpole as butterfly : _____

_____

2. rattlesnake : alligator as _____ : salamander

_____

3. sedimentary : sandstone as metamorphic : _____

_____

4. astronomy : star as paleontology : _____

_____

5. lungs : respiration as _____ : circulation

_____

6. snake : cold-blooded as _____ : warm-blooded

_____

7. Mercury : Venus as Uranus : _____

_____

8. avalanche : snow as glacier : _____

_____

9. Curie : radium as Fleming : _____

_____

10. centimeter : inch as _____ : quart

_____

SCIENCE   Verbal-Linguistic Intelligence

Eponyms

Sometimes people's contributions to science are so important that the people become an eponym. That is, the people have their contribution named after them. One example is Gabriel Fahrenheit, who gave his name to the Fahrenheit thermometer. Research the people below. Write the contribution that is named after them.

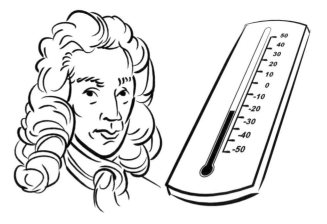

1. Ernst Mach	
2. Rudolf Diesel	
3. André Marie Ampère	
4. Lord Kelvin (William Thomson)	
5. Anders Celsius	
6. Alessandro Volta	
7. Pierre Curie	
8. Georg Simon Ohm	
9. Sequoya (George Guess)	

SCIENCE
Verbal-Linguistic Intelligence

Name _____

All About Matter

Use the clues and the words in the Word Box to complete the puzzle.

Word Box

matter	weight	molecules
mass	solubility	conductivity
density	atom	liquid

ACROSS
2. the ability of matter to conduct heat or electricity
4. objects that move from the earth into outer space lose this
5. the amount of mass for each unit of volume
7. the smallest particle of an element that can exist alone or in combination
8. atoms form larger particles called

DOWN
1. the ability of one kind of matter to dissolve in another
3. has no shape of its own
6. the substance of which all things are made
8. a measure of inertia

Verbal-Linguistic Intelligence

Masterpiece Masters

Expose your students to great works of art by famous artists. Provide students with books of artists' work or visit the web sites listed below and read about each artist. Have students write reports about their chosen artist.

Cassatt, Cezanne, Gauguin, Homer, Manet, Monet, Munch, Picasso, Pissarro, Rembrandt, Renoir, Sisley, and Toulouse-Lautrec—
http://lonestar.texas.net/~mharden/artchive/
(Once at this site, navigate to the desired artchive.)

> da Vinci— http://sunsite.unc.edu/wm/paint/auth/vinci
>
> Goya—http://www.imageone.com/goya/parasol.html
>
> Rembrandt—http://sunsite.unc.edu/wm/paint/auth/rembrandt/
>
> van Gogh—http://www.iem.ac.ru/wm/paint/auth/gogh

Being an Art Critic

Encourage students to use their linguistic intelligence to critique a work of art. Show a reproduction or work of art to the students. Tell the students to pretend that they work for an art magazine as an art critic. Discuss the major components of art: point, line, shape, color, value, pattern, form, space. Have the students brainstorm a list of words or phrases about the work of art. Pose questions to get students to think about similarities, contrasts, and continuities or rhythms in color, shape, or size. For example: Is there a color or shape repeated? Are objects different sizes or shapes? Is the composition balanced? Encourage students to think about and list the feelings, ideas, or emotions the work of art evokes. Ask students to think about what supports their hypothesis. Then share with the students a few art reviews from art books or magazines. Discuss how the art critics analyzed and interpreted the artwork. Then, using their lists, have the students each write a paragraph about the work of art.

Logical-Mathematical Intelligence

Color and Design

Here is an activity to help the logical-mathematical student learn about color. Give each student a 9" x 12" sheet of white construction paper, a pencil, a paintbrush, water, black paint, white paint, and two primary colors of paint. Tell the students their task is to make a design with three overlapping shapes. Have the students sketch a design. Then tell them to use one primary color for their main shape and the other primary color for the two overlapping shapes, creating secondary colors where they overlap. Have the students add black and white to both primary colors to create a range of tints and shades. Frame the artwork and display in the classroom.

Asymmetrical Pictures

Show the students various works of art that are asymmetrically balanced, with equal visual weight on either side of its axis, but not symmetrical. Give the students a large sheet of construction paper, scraps of construction paper of various colors, scissors, and glue. Have the students each cut a variety of sizes and colors of various shapes. Ask the students to use these shapes to create an asymmetrical design that is balanced. Discuss each design and identify the balance. Then frame each design and display them in the classroom or hallway.

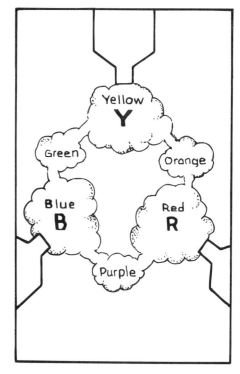

Bodily-Kinesthetic Intelligence

Mighty Casey

Have students develop their bodily-kinesthetic intelligence by performing the poem "Casey at the Bat," by Ernest L. Thayer (Atheneum, 1995). Give each student a copy of the poem. Let the students read the poem to themselves. Then have the students reread the poem and name various characters they could be, such as Casey, the umpire, the pitcher, Flynn, or Blake. Have the students think about the actions they would use to pantomime these various characters. Then ask for volunteers to narrate the poem. (You may have one student narrate the entire poem, two students narrate by alternating each stanza, or thirteen students narrate by each reading one stanza.) Ask for volunteers to play the character of Casey, the umpire, the pitcher, and any other characters. The remaining students can play the part of the patrons. Let students switch parts and repeat the performance. As an extension, let the class perform the play for another class.

Gesture Drawing

Explain to the class that gesture drawing is a drawing technique using quickly drawn lines that create a sense of energy and motion. The object of the exercise is to draw as fast as possible to capture the energy of the subject. Each drawing is created in 60 seconds, and the pen should be moving continually within this time period, without leaving the paper.

Gesture Drawing Directions:

Materials: Construction paper, pen

1. Choose a volunteer to stand where she or he can be see by everyone in the class. The volunteer should strike a pose that conveys action, such as running, dancing, pitching a baseball, etc.

2. Have the students quickly draw the overall shape of the person. Their pens should never leave the paper as they draw. They are trying to draw an outline rather than capture details such as facial features, fingers, or hair.

3. Tell the students to start drawing faster. And even faster!

4. After one minute, their drawings are complete. Begin the procedure with a different model.

Visual-Spatial Intelligence

whole

half

quarter

eighth

sixteenth

thirty-second

sixty-fourth

A Bird's Eye View

Students can exercise their imagination to do this art project. Tell them to think of a place that is very familiar to them, such as their bedroom, outside of their home including house and yard, the classroom, or a favorite place. Ask children to pretend they are hovering about this place looking down on it. Try to imagine what the scene would look like. Allow students to choose a medium to render the scene.

Create a Class Mascot

Prior to this lesson, divide the class into groups of five. Each group will create a class mascot. The groups should each chose a medium they would like to work with—paint, clay, found-object sculpture, wood, etc. Encourage students to name the mascot and write a short tale about how it was chosen.

Musical Concentration

This center activity allows students to use spatial intelligence to learn about music. Make a set of musical matching cards on index cards. Make a card for each of the following musical notes: whole, 1/2, 1/4, 1/8, 1/16, 1/32, 1/64. Make the corresponding cards with the notes on them as shown at left.

Also make matching instrument cards and their names. Be sure to include unfamiliar instruments such as a lute, a sousaphone, a mandolin, or a sitar.

Also make musician portrait cards and their corresponding names, using classical composers, such as Mozart and Schubert, as well as modern figures such as Aretha Franklin and Bob Dylan.

Be sure students hear the music represented before playing the game. Place these cards at a center. To play, two or more students place the cards face down on a table. One student turns over two cards to try to get a match. If the student is successful, then he or she gets another turn. Otherwise, it is the next person's turn.

Musical Intelligence

Song and Dance

For this song and dance activity, students create a dance to a common song. Divide the students into small groups of four to five. Play a song with a simple lively beat several times for the class. Let the students move to the rhythm of the music. Tell the students that each group is to create their own dance for the song. Give students ample time to create and practice their dance. Keep playing the song as the students are working so they can move to the rhythm. Have each group perform their dance. Students will be surprised at the various interpretations. Allow them to choose their own songs to choreograph also.

Interpersonal Intelligence

Color Wheel Mosaic

This art project will give students an opportunity to see the relationship of one color to another as they are positioned on a color wheel. In groups, students will create a mural-sized mosaic of the color wheel. Each student will be assigned a color and will create this portion of the mosaic.

Begin by displaying a large color wheel. Point out the primary colors–yellow, red, and blue–and secondary colors–orange, purple, and green. Explain that between these six colors are intermediate colors–yellow-orange, red-orange, red-violet, blue-violet, blue-green, and yellow-green. Complementary colors are colors that are found directly opposite each other on the wheel. Pairs of complementary colors are red and green, for example, and orange and blue.

Distribute the **The Color Wheel** worksheet on page 65 to the class and have

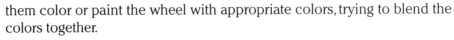
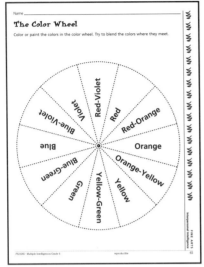

page 65

them color or paint the wheel with appropriate colors, trying to blend the colors together.

Before starting the project below, review the process of creating a mosaic with the class. Explain that historically mosaics were made with tile, stone, or glass pieces called tesserae. Display pictures of mosaics found in mosques, walls, or furniture. Jewelry and tile floors are also created with the mosaic technique.

Directions for a Color Wheel Mosaic:

Materials: paper, watercolor, tempera paint or crayons, glue, scissors, glitter glue (optional)

1. Draw a large circle on butcher paper. On the inside of the circle mark lightly with pencil the 12 sections of the color wheel. Put the color wheel on a table where it is accessible. (More than one color wheel may be necessary depending on the number of students in the class.)

2. Each student should choose a primary or secondary color of the wheel.

3. On white paper, students should draw a triangle the same size as a section of the color wheel. The paper should be colored with either crayons or paint before it is cut into small pieces. Each student will be creating a piece of the wheel, making sure that his or her color blends with the colors bordering it. Therefore, more than one color will be used by each student. For example, a student who chooses the color green will color his or her section green to yellow-green on one side, and green to blue-green on the other side.

4. Once the paper has been colored, it should be cut into small pieces.

5. Students can be working simultaneously to glue their tesserae to the wheel. Point out to students that they must leave room for other students to intersperse their tesserae around the borders of their colors so that the colors will blend nicely.

6. Glitter can be added to the finished spectrum.

Improvisation

Here's an improvisation activity to develop students' interpersonal intelligence. Prior to the activity, collect no-longer-used clothes, hats, scarves, and such accessories as jewelry, handbags, canes, and briefcases. Store the garments in one box and the accessories in another.

Divide the students into groups. Explain that in improvisation a central theme is given and the performers begin acting out this theme. They must be quick thinking and able to pick up on clues from their fellow actors. Tell the students that they are going to be going to an amusement park. Have them think about their characters. Pose questions to help the students form their characters. For example, are they a worker or patron; are they alone or with a friend or family members; or are they young or old? Let students choose garments and accessories if they want. Then allow groups to perform without

an audience to become comfortable with themselves and each other. Then have the class observe the performances. Other themes to perform are: being at the mall, a baseball game, a concert, the dentist's office, or on a cruise ship.

Pop-up Cards

Distribute the **Pop-ups** student worksheet on page 66 worksheet to your students. Allow them to make the cards and give them to the person of their choice. The object to pop up from the card can be made from a construction paper cut out, a drawing, painting or print, a photograph or an image cut from a magazine.

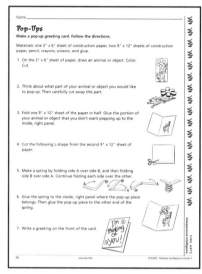

page 66

Intrapersonal Intelligence

Musical Pictures

For this activity you will need tapes or CDs of various types of music, such as jazz, rock, country, or classical. Give each student a large sheet of white construction paper, paints, paintbrush, and water. Ask the students if colors and brushstrokes can describe music. What colors are loud or soft? What kind of brushstrokes describe the music? Have the student divide the paper into sections for each type of music you will play. Then play one of the music selections. Have the students listen to the music and think about what colors and brushstrokes the music evokes. Have the students use various colors and brushstrokes to paint in one section. Repeat with the other musical selections. After, have students try to match their classmates art work to each musical piece.

It's Me

Encourage students to activate their intrapersonal intelligence through making collages. Have the students create personal collages. Give each student a 9" x 12" sheet of construction paper, old magazines, scissors, and glue. Tell them to cut out pictures of things (including words) that reflect what they like about themselves. Have them glue these pictures and words onto the paper to create a picture of themselves. When they've finished the project, have students write an essay explaining the choices they made in creating the collage.

Daydreaming

Daydreaming can be used as a form of relaxation and to develop intrapersonal intelligence. On a day when students need a quieting-down time, suggest they close their eyes and imagine themselves at a beach. Speaking slowly and quietly, tell them to picture themselves walking on the

shore. What do they encounter? What do they hear? What do they smell and see? Give students time to bring up their own images after each question. It's important to imagine yourself continually moving during this exercise so that the mind is constantly engaged. Tell students to put themselves in other settings and to travel slowly through the imaginary environment. The point is to travel down a path rather than stay stationary. Visualizing a process, such as gardening or baking cookies, can also be calming.

Naturalist Intelligence

Leaf Prints

This printing activity activates the students' naturalist intelligence. Give each student a brown lunch sack. Take the students on a walk outside. Have the student collect various leaves from the ground. Encourage them to collect as many different shapes as possible and to choose ones that have clear patterns. After the walk, have the students examine their leaves. Get them to focus on the patterns, lines, and shapes. Give each student a 12" x 18" sheet of white construction, water, and a paintbrush. Let the students choose one to three colors of paint. Ask the students to paint over the rough side of a leaf with paint, press the leaf down on the paper, and carefully peel off the leaf. Continue using other leaves and colors. Encourage the students to overlap the leaf prints. After the prints are dry, frame and display them in the classroom or hallway. Or use them with the following activity, Make Animal Tracks.

Make Animal Tracks

Ask each student to choose an animal and research what its tracks look like. Don't forget animals such as dinosaurs, snakes, and those that drag their tail. Students should note that front tracks of animals are often different than hind tracks. A good reference for tracks is *Secrets of a Wildlife Watcher*, by Jim Arnosky (Beech Tree, 1991). Have students make tracks on long pieces of paper.

Track stamps can be made with a raw potato. Draw the track on the potato half and cut away the excess potato until the track protrudes about a quarter inch. This can be inked and used as a stamp.

Each student should label his or her track. The finished products can be attached to each other and hung in the classroom for display. Drawings of leaves, rocks, flowers, etc., can be added to the track mural to make it more lifelike and decorative.

The Color Wheel

Color or paint the colors in the color wheel. Try to blend the colors where they meet.

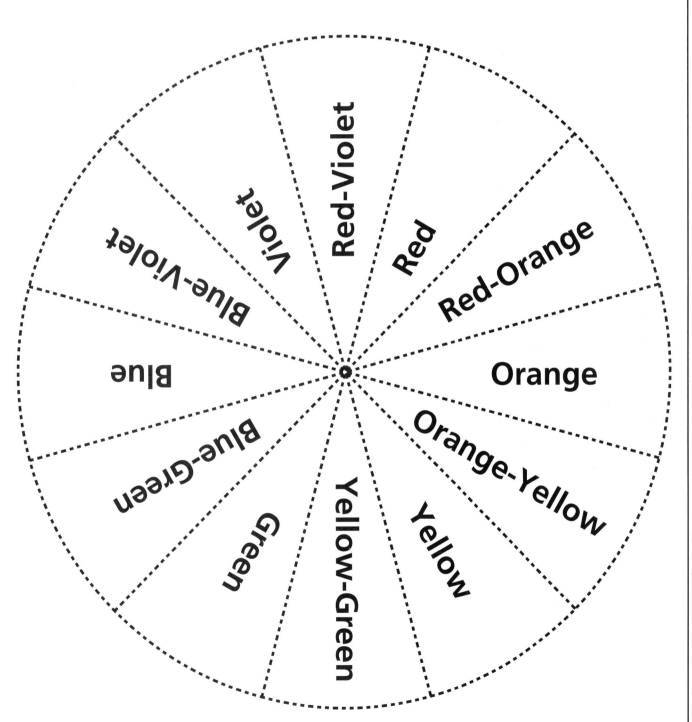

Pop-Ups

Make a pop-up greeting card. Follow the directions.

Materials: one 3" x 6" sheet of construction paper, two 9" x 12" sheets of construction paper, pencil, crayons, scissors, and glue.

1. On the 3" x 6" sheet of paper, draw an animal or object. Color. Cut.

2. Think about what part of your animal or object you would like to pop-up. Then carefully cut away this part.

3. Fold one 9" x 12" sheet of the paper in half. Glue the portion of your animal or object that you don't want popping up to the inside, right panel.

4. Cut the following L-shape from the second 9" x 12" sheet of paper:

5. Make a spring by folding side A over side B, and then folding side B over side A. Continue folding each side over the other.

6. Glue the spring to the inside, right panel where the pop-up piece belongs. Then glue the pop-up piece to the other end of the spring.

7. Write a greeting on the front of the card.

reproducible

FS23285 · Multiple Intelligences Grade 6

FINE ARTS
Interpersonal Intelligence

Verbal-Linguistic Intelligence

Ice Hockey Action

Collect several ice hockey articles from various newspapers. Divide the students into groups of four. Give each group an article, a 9-by-12-inch sheet of white construction paper, a sheet of writing paper, and a pencil. Have each group divide the construction paper into four boxes and label *nouns, verbs, adjectives,* and *adverbs.* Let the groups read their article and identify any nouns, verbs, adjectives, or adverbs that are in the article. Then enter these words in the correct box. Next, have each group write descriptive sentences about ice hockey or write a poem that captures the fast action of a hockey match. Encourage students to use the words from the various boxes. Let each group share their writings with the class.

Honor Your Partner

Square dancing is an excellent way to activate students' linguistic intelligence while getting physical exercise. Divide the students into groups of eight. Have each group form four sets of two. Teach the students some of the basic square dancing moves, such as allemande left, swing your partner, promenade, etc. Then play a tape of square dancing music and call out various dance moves, or play a tape that includes a caller. Tell students that they must listen carefully to the directions as they are called.

Vocabulary Workout

Stimulate your students' vocabulary while they learn the rules of tennis with the student worksheet on page 74, **Some Racket!** Students can create their own racket with a wire coat hanger and a nylon stocking. Bend the triangular section of the hanger into a diamond shape, then stretch the stocking over the diamond. Secure the the stocking with a rubber band. Use a foam ball or balloon to play.

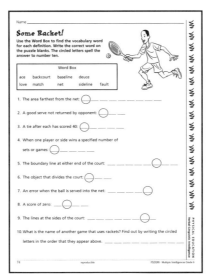

page 74

Logical-Mathematical Intelligence

Necessary Skills

Explain to the students that they are to interview three school athletes or coaches in various sports to find out what skills players need, such as speed, agility, and reach. Have the class as a group prepare a questionnaire in advance so that they ask similar questions of each player. Encourage students to include questions that involve issues of morale, confidence, and team spirit. Duplicate enough questionnaires so that each student receives three. After the interviews, have the class prepare a chart of their results on a large sheet of chart paper. Use this chart to have the students compare and contrast the sports. Discuss what qualities the various athletes share and how they differ. Ask how they might apply those qualities to other activities, both personal and those that involve group activities.

Design a Game

Here are some problem-solving activities to develop logical-mathematical intelligence and physical skills. Divide the students into groups of four to five and give them the problems below to solve. Let each group share their games with the class.

- Give each group a ball, two hoops, and a cone. Tell the students to make up a game using all of the items.

- Give each group three beanbags and four hoops. Tell the students to make up a game using all of the items.

- Give each group a beanbag and a hoop. Tell the students to invent three different ways to pick up the beanbag using different parts of their body and then throw it into the hoop.

- Give each group a frisbee and a jump rope. Tell the students to make up a game using these two items.

To further stimulate the students logical-mathematical intelligence, have them complete the **Sports Analogies** worksheet on page 75.

Softball Throw

Here's an activity to develop students' throwing skills and logical-mathematical intelligence. For each group, place five boxes with openings of various widths in a row. Label the boxes with numbers 1–5, with the smallest opening labeled *five*, the largest *one*, and so on. Give each student a softball. Place your students into pairs, and give each pair a pencil and sheet of paper. Have the two students stand approximately 10 feet away from the boxes. Have one student throw his or her softball into one of the boxes. Then

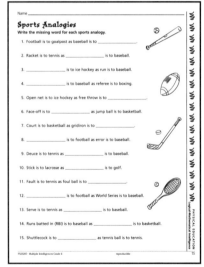

page 75

have the partner throw his or her softball into one of the boxes. Add the numbers to get their team score. (If the ball misses a box, the score is zero.) Have them write their score on a sheet of paper. Now, let another pair throw their softballs and total their score. Continue playing, having teams keep a running score. The team that first scores 30 is the winner. Note, the team cannot score over 30. For example, if the team has 28, they will have to throw one softball into the box marked "2" or throw two softballs each into the box marked "1."

Bodily-Kinesthetic Intelligence

What an Obstacle!

This bodily-kinesthetic intelligence activity increases students' overall fitness in a fun and challenging way. Prior to the class, design and set up an obstacle course. Examples may be jumping through hoops, crawling through a tunnel, dribbling a ball around cones, walking across a balance beam, climbing a rope, or jumping over hurdles. First, walk the students through the course. Then have each student go through the course and time him or her. Then have the students go through the course again to see if they can improve their times. You may wish to have students keep a record of their times. Once a month, have each student complete the course. Students will be able to monitor their progress and see improvement in their endurance.

Soccer Skills

Students can develop their passing skills, defensive skills, and kicking accuracy with this activity. Divide the students into groups of three, and give each group a soccer ball. Place two cones approximately six feet apart at the end of the field or gymnasium for each team. Have one student on each team be the goalie and stand between the two cones. Explain to the goalies that for this exercise they must stay between the two cones and try to block the ball. Have the other two students stand on the opposite side of the field or gymnasium. These two students are to practice moving the ball down the field between one another and try to make a goal by kicking the ball between the two cones. After several attempts, have the goalie switch places

with a kicker. Continue until every player has been the goalie. Next, have one group member be the goalie, one the kicker, and the other a defender. Explain that the goalie's objective remains the same. However, one group member brings the ball down and attempts a goal (the kicker) and the other member attempts to steal the ball from this person (defender). Switch roles after several attempts. Continue until each group member has played all three positions.

Visual-Spatial Intelligence

Sports Designs

Break the class up into small groups of three to five students. Ask the groups to design various items for school teams. They could design T-shirts to be hand painted or silk screened. They could also design banners, posters for upcoming sports events, team uniforms, or clothing for a mascot.

Musical Intelligence

Musical Motivations

Use students' musical intelligence to get them motivated about physical fitness. Ask students to think of people they know who work out regularly. Suggest that they survey three people to find out if they listen to music while working out. If they do, have them find out what music they use. As a class, tally the results of the surveys, creating a chart that shows the titles of the pieces used, the type of exercise it is used with, and a brief description of the type of music. Now, have the students bring in music on the chart as well as their own selections. During class, play this music to motivate students to get physically fit.

Aerobic Routines

Have the students work in pairs to develop an aerobic routine. Tell the students that they are to develop a five-minute aerobic routine for the class. Have the class brainstorm possible actions the routine may entail, such as leg kicks, jumping jacks, jogging forward or backwards, or arm curls while jogging in place. Encourage students to make up some of their own moves also. The pairs should find music and choreograph an aerobic routine that

Target Heart Rates

Age	Beats Per Minute
9	148–211
10	147–210
11	146–209
12	145–208

goes with it. Have two of the groups develop a warm-up and a cool-down routine. Let the pairs practice for several periods until they are ready to teach it to the class. Then each group should teach their routine. The warm-up team should teach theirs first. Once everyone has taught their routine, a gym period can be devoted to aerobics.

Take note of heart rates during aerobics classes. See the chart above. Check that students' heart rates are within these ranges after five minutes of exercise.

Interpersonal Intelligence

Coaching Skills

Invite a coach to visit and discuss the techniques he or she uses to develop a team. For example, how does he or she handle such things as rules, skills development, teamwork, attitude, praise, and helpful criticism? Have the students interview the coach with questions they have prepared in advance. Later, have students summarize what they learned. Let individual students act as assistant coaches during a physical education class or on a one-on-one basis. Then have them write a paragraph about their experience. Encourage them to include what they learned about working with other people and what they learned about themselves.

Group Triathlon

The following three activities are for groups of students and require communication and cooperation. The activities can be timed and each considered a portion of a triathlon. Groups can compete against each other for a final prize. Make sure students are provided with opportunities to practice before the competition begins.

Untie the Knot

In a large, cleared area, ask groups of students to join hands with their group members to create a large knot of people. Students can cross arms above and below classmates' arms. They may also twist their bodies around and step over classmates' joined hands. When the knot is complete, students must work together to "untie" the knot without releasing hands at any time. Encourage students to move under and step over other students' hands. The goal is to end up with one large circle of students holding hands.

Up You Go!

Have each group create a human pyramid. Students can create the pyramid levels by crouching on their hands and knees. The base level should consist of four students on hands and knees. Be sure to choose "spotters" to help prevent injury. Have the groups build their pyramids more than once to improve their team skills and increase their times.

Hoop Relay

Give each team a large plastic hoop. Have the teams line up at one end of the gymnasium or field. At the other end of the gymnasium or field, place a cone opposite each team. Have the teams form pairs within their teams. Then have a pair from each team run down to the cone and back with both people inside the hoop. At the finish line, the pair must pass its hoop on to the next pair. That pair continues the race and passes the hoop to the next pair. The first team to finish wins.

Intrapersonal Intelligence

P. E. Journal

Keeping a physical education journal can encourage students to set their own physical education goals and monitor their progress, as well as make physical education more personal.

- For each physical education unit, have the students set a personal goal. For example, a student may want to become a better ball handler or team player in basketball. Help them think of ways they could improve. Encourage them in class to work on this goal. Have them makes notes on their progress in their journal.

- Have students write about their long-range goals in the journals, also. What activities do they hope to do during the next year? In five years? When they are sixty-five?

- Have students take their heart rate before, during, and after any physical activity. Ask the students to keep a chart in their journal noting rates and how they felt. Encourage students to reflect on and evaluate their heart rates. As the students become more physically fit, they will see their heart rates lower and their stamina improve.

- Are there any sports figures, local or world-class, students would like to emulate? Encourage them to write to or about these people.

- Have students write about how being physically fit can help them in other areas of their lives. How can it positively effect their social lives, schoolwork, personal goals, etc.?

- Have students write a creative visualization of themselves performing the activity of their choice. They should write in the present tense and first person. For example: *My muscles feel warm and limber from my warm-up activity. I am putting on my helmet. Now I am getting on my bike. I pedal up a hill...*

Gymnastics

A gymnastic unit is an excellent opportunity to help develop students' intrapersonal intelligence. At the end of your gymnastics unit, have a gymnastics performance. Let the students decide on the type of performance they would like to give, such as the balance beam, a floor routine, or the uneven bars. Tell the students that their routine should be approximately 2 to 5 minutes. Encourage them to select music for their performance. Give the students ample time to develop and practice their routines. Then invite parents or other classes to attend the performance.

Naturalist Intelligence

Outdoors Project

Students can create a personal project based on an outdoor activity that they enjoy doing on their own. Some activities to choose from are: hiking, fishing, camping, bird watching, cross-country running, skiing. Have the students create a list of goals they'd like to meet in this activity. (Parental supervision will be needed for some activities.) Students can also include any of the following in their project: safety tips for the sports or activity, instructions on how to perform a task or skill related to the activity, a map, a photo essay, or a journal. Have students present their reports to the class.

Some Racket!

Use the Word Box to find the vocabulary word for each definition. Write the correct word on the puzzle blanks. The circled letters spell the answer to number ten.

Word Box			
ace	backcourt	baseline	deuce
love	match	net	sideline	fault

1. The area farthest from the net: ◯__ __ __ __ __ __ __ __

2. A good serve not returned by opponent: ◯__ __

3. A tie after each has scored 40: ◯__ __ __ __

4. When one player or side wins a specified number of sets or games: ◯__ __ __ __

5. The boundary line at either end of the court: __ __ __ __ __ ◯__ __

6. The object that divides the court: ◯__ __

7. An error when the ball is served into the net: __ __ __ __ ◯

8. A score of zero: __ ◯__ __

9. The lines at the sides of the court: __ __ __ __ __ __ ◯__

10. What is the name of another game that uses rackets? Find out by writing the circled letters in the order that they appear above. __ __ __ __ __ __ __ __ __ __

Name _____

Sports Analogies

Write the missing word for each sports analogy.

1. Football is to goalpost as baseball is to _____.

2. Racket is to tennis as _____ is to baseball.

3. _____ is to ice hockey as run is to baseball.

4. _____ is to baseball as referee is to boxing.

5. Open net is to ice hockey as free throw is to _____.

6. Face-off is to _____ as jump ball is to basketball.

7. Court is to basketball as gridiron is to _____.

8. _____ is to football as error is to baseball.

9. Deuce is to tennis as _____ is to baseball.

10. Stick is to lacrosse as _____ is to golf.

11. Fault is to tennis as foul ball is to _____.

12. _____ is to football as World Series is to baseball.

13. Serve is to tennis as _____ is to baseball.

14. Runs batted in (RBI) is to baseball as _____ is to basketball.

15. Shuttlecock is to _____ as tennis ball is to tennis.

PHYSICAL EDUCATION
Logical-Mathematical Intelligence

ANSWERS

Page 20: Anagrams

1. words	2. meal
3. wolf	4. pots
5. sneak	6. tow
7. sure	8. ache
9. won	10. slime
11. time	12. lose
13. veer	14. below
15. file	

Page 44: Word Fractions

A. ape	B. rent
C. gram	D. me
E. try	F. eel
G. lane	H. actions
I. numb	J. even
K. hall	L. fact

Page 46: Beside the Point

A. 5.79	B. 8.67
C. 0.99	D. 4782
E. 375	F. 6.6
G. 116	H. 0.329
I. 99	J. 6.8
K. 4.8	L. 89.4
M. 37	N. 33.32
O. 8.8125	P. 2.4

Page 55: Science Analogies

1. caterpillar; A frog develops from a tadpole. A butterfly develops from a caterpillar.
2. toad; Rattlesnake and alligator belong to the same animal family. A toad and a salamander are in the same family.
3. quartz; Sandstone is a kind of sedimentary rock; quartz is a kind of metamorphic rock.
4. dinosaur; Astronomy is the study of stars and paleontology is the study of dinosaurs.
5. heart; The lungs control respiration, and the heart controls circulation.
6. monkey; A snake is a cold-blooded animal. A monkey is a warm-blooded animal.
7. Pluto; Mercury and Venus are inner planets. Uranus and Pluto are outer planets.
8. ice; An avalanche is moving snow. A glacier is moving ice.
9. penicillin; Curie discovered radium. Fleming discovered penicillin.
10. liter; Centimeter and inch are metric and standard measurements of length. Liter and quart are metric and standard measurements for volume.

Page 56: Eponyms

1. Mach number, used as a measure of speed
2. diesel engine
3. ampere, used to measure the flow of an electric current
4. Kelvin scale, a temperature scale that begins at absolute zero
5. Celsius scale of temperature
6. Volt, a unit of electrical measurement
7. Curie, a unit of radioactivity
8. Ohm, a unit of electrical resistance
9. Sequoia, huge California tree

Page 57: All About Matter

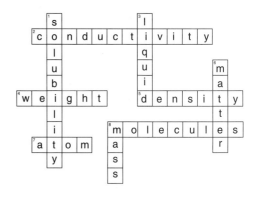

Page 74: Some Racket

1. backcourt
2. ace
3. deuce
4. match
5. baseline
6. net
7. fault
8. love
9. sideline
10. badminton

Page 75: Sports Analogies

1. home plate
2. bat
3. skate
4. umpire
5. basketball
6. ice hockey
7. football
8. fumble
9. tie
10. club
11. baseball
12. Super Bowl
13. pitch
14. assists
15. badminton